Dancing With Wolves

Harold Williams Jr.

ISBN: 978-1545449455

Published by: Kelly Publishing 2017

Dedication

I dedicate this book to my loving and supportive wife, Jonniece. Despite the past, she always affirms who I am in Christ. She is truly my rib and a mighty woman of God, in her own right. Thank you for believing in me even when I struggled within myself. Thank you for your constant words of affirmation.

To my children both naturally and spiritually, I pledge to honor you as my sons and daughters and never to allow you to go through this abuse.

I dedicate this to all sheep that have been hurt or misused at the hands of a wolf. Despite how you have felt, your wholeness is made manifest through the stripes of Jesus Christ.

I also dedicate this to the righteous leaders that have played a vital part in my life (Apostle Steven Hilton, Dr. Melodye Hilton, and Apostle Louis Dickens). Thanks for showing me the true essence of spiritual love and encouraging me to complete this project.

Table of Contents

Foreword

My heart was riveted as well as broken as I read Harold Williams' true life story. His life events provide an earned platform to reveal a life of fear versus pure love, faith versus works, and healthy influence versus wounded leadership. My personal judgments are constructed through a justice-minded leadership lens. Justice-minded leaders use their influence and position for the good of others as they give of themselves unreservedly living for a higher cause. Many have screamed "*abuse of leadership*" because they had a self-focused agenda, their painful past experience was projected onto others, or their entitled pursuit of benefits outweighed their willingness to work hard within partnership. But for Harold, and many others, they have or are now living through the hell of *Dancing with Wolves* in shepherd's clothing. Injustice is an abuse of power using others to benefit self and raping the identity of others to wear damaged clothes of success and facade of spirituality. Whether consciously aware or not, these individuals prey upon the hurting; they know that their vulnerability will be fertile soil allowing injustice to be hidden behind the veil of insecurity, fear, or pride. *Hurt people hurt people* is a valid statement.

Neuroscience reveals an individual's need for love and validation. Human nature will expend large amounts of emotional energy trying to manipulate circumstances or people to meet their fear and shame-based needs. Everything we do through fear perverts the purity of what we do and the expression of who we uniquely are. Within the pages of *Dancing with Wolves,* Harold Williams writes with an authentic vulnerability as he shares the *slippery slope* to self-protective hypocrisy. He learned to fit into a model that propagated spiritual and social injustice that reproduced oppression rather than the freedom God has intended for His sons and daughters.

Harold Williams' journey to freedom will provide you with indicators of a faulty system and unhealthy leadership as well as the reactions and outcomes of its members. His story of courage will provide a testimonial road map to realize your value and step into spiritual and emotional health.

One truth that is true for all of us is that our Father God defines us--not man or our experience. As you read, I believe you will look through the lens of internal freedom empowering you to interpret your past with thankfulness, your present with courage, and your future with hope!

Dr. Melodye Hilton

Author: Higher Living Leadership

Introduction

Dancing with Wolves

Did you hear about the young man that got caught up with "Dancing with Wolves?" He was young, gifted and innocent, but vulnerable. He was rejected by his own peers, father, and ministry leaders. So, he was looking to connect with people that would be there for him and potentially fill the voids.

When you are vulnerable, you are opened to anyone that is going to show you love and attention. So, this young man went through a season at the church he grew up in, and he noticed that he didn't fit it. The church was more of a traditional, religious church but he had personal experiences with the Holy Spirit that contradicted the belief systems of the pastor and the church body. He still was faithful to the church and even became a minister on staff. As he matured in God, the gifts of the Holy Spirit would manifest through him in a major, impactful way. Some were open to it and others weren't. He could tell the ones that weren't. The young man kept pressing, but the rejection from the people began to weigh on him. He believed they loved him, but they just couldn't relate to his spiritual experiences. He began to pray that God would allow him to leave the church and go to where he felt was a better type of church that believed in the gifts and power of God.

The young man was invited to preach a revival at a Pentecostal church. He had never preached at this type of church, so he was excited about the opportunity. He went and preached and had a great time being able to flow freely under the anointing of the Holy Spirit. After the revival, he felt the need to go back and visit that church. So, he went back a few times and enjoyed the word, worship, and the fellowship. A little while later, he joined the ministry and became a minister on staff.

Months and months went by and the young man felt like he was in heaven. He was so excited about the opportunity to be in the church that he missed some obvious things that were right in front of his eyes. He never even took a second thought that this ministry seemed a little too perfect. As time progressed, he noticed there were a lot of people in that church that were going through divorces. Families were falling apart. He then noticed that the organ player/minister of music was very flamboyant and had mannerisms of a woman. Then, he experienced for himself the worst thing. The minister of music made a pass at him right in the church. How could it be that a powerful church like this was allowing a homosexual to lead the people into worship? It gets worse. He, as well as other members of the church, went to the senior leadership about the need for the minister of music to step down until he went through deliverance, but that notion was ignored. Why? The obvious was heartbreaking, the minister of music was gifted and his gifting in the eyes of the leadership overrode his need for deliverance. This within itself was some dangerous stuff.

The young man stayed at the church believing that there would be change and he found himself echoing the words of the leadership "no church is perfect." Listen, when people repeatedly announce this, it's because they are trying to cover up their lack or desire for true deliverance.

Of course, gossip went around the church. The reason the pastor didn't address this type of behavior was because he was in the lifestyle. The young man wished with all of his heart that he had never joined the church, but at this point did not leave because he felt that God had sent him there. *There is still more.....*

The young man thought I can either go back to the church that I grew up in where no one understands me or I can stay where I am a place of acceptance, pray about the situation and keep it moving. He even put a charge on himself that he would be the agent of change and would bring about the deliverance that the church needed. So, that is what he did. He stayed there. But in the midst of staying, little did he know that he was about to encounter some real wolves and he was unable to execute the change that he tried to convince himself that he was capable of bringing.

One day, there was a fellowship gathering of all of the churches in the region under his leader. At this time, he served as an adjutant or armor bearer. He was asked to serve one of the bishops. You know that religious stuff...carry his bag, get him some juice and wipe his face if he sweats, but no one told him what else he might be asked to do. He was preparing the "Man of God" the Bishop, The Right Reverend; to go out into the service when the Bishop cornered him and asked the young, oblivious man could he "have him?" Yep, that's what he said. He wanted to have sex with this young man. He invited him to his house, offered to take him shopping, etc. He was an older man and was accustomed to using his money to lure young men for sexual favors. This bishop was a seasoned wolf, and the young man was his intended prey. The young man resisted his offers and advances and insisted that he regain focus and go into the service immediately. They entered the service like nothing happened and the bishop preached the house down. There were praise breaks, people falling out and don't forget the infamous hour-long offering where the preacher becomes an auctioneer throwing out different amounts and the people jump up to throw the offering at his feet. "I need 20 people with 200 hundred dollars to sow today. Now, I need 10 people with 50 dollars to sow." A straight up scheme to fatten his pockets. It sounded like craziness to me.

After the service, the young man asked God, "How could this be?" Bishop came at me like this, but yet he goes out in front of the church and performs and the people buy it. This seemed like religion at its best. So, the young man left the church that evening headed home and called a good friend that was also in ministry. He told his good friend what happened between him and Bishop. To his surprise, his good friend said, "Yeah that's how Bishop is and everyone knows. Even though he is married, he and his wife live in separate homes and put on a show like they are ok." The young man said, "Well, why hasn't anyone said anything? Why hasn't he been sat down from his ministry?" He advised, "Because many have been sworn to secrecy and if you want to move up in the organization you better keep your mouth shut."

So, the young man throughout the years, kept his mouth shut until he became so numb to the reality of the strange situation. He knew what was going on but wanted a position and wanted to feel apart. Hey, doors were opening, so why not buckle up and enjoy the ride.

He began to notice that the minister of music and the Bishop were not the only ones with deep roots of perversion but also others he got close to in the church and organization. He had heard of churches pulling out of the organization because of the perversion, but he kept on trucking and ignored it. The reality was that he was dancing with the wolves of religiosity and if he wasn't careful, he would soon fall prey to the religious wolf as well. As he continued to serve the men of God, he watched the deception, manipulation and even control that these leaders would exemplify.

Eventually, he fell into the perversion, the control, and the manipulation. He began to develop ungodly love triangles with men and woman of the organization. As he did this, his reputation as a mighty man of God became, "Oh, he is just like the rest of them." He continued in this until he had enough. It was almost six years later. He had a wake-up call from the Holy Spirit. If he didn't shift from all of this, death would be his destiny. After that awakening of dancing with the wolves, he decided to leave that church. Of course, he received the curses of you will never make it and you are going to be cursed if you leave. All the people that supposedly loved and supported him now gave him the cold shoulder. The rejection that he was so familiar with was back. Remember, he had danced with the wolves and when he got out of step and out of sync with the wolves, they turned and attacked. So, you have this bloody victim with no hope for his future.

Ezekiel 22:23-31 23And the word of the LORD came unto me, saying, 24Son of man, say unto her, Thou art the land that is not cleansed, nor rained upon in the day of indignation. 25There is a conspiracy of her prophets in the midst thereof, like a roaring lion ravening the prey; they have devoured souls; they have taken the treasure and precious things; they have made her many widows in the midst thereof. 26Her priests have violated my law, and have profaned mine holy things: they have put no difference between the holy and profane, neither have they shewed difference between the unclean and the clean, and have hidden their eyes from my Sabbaths, and I am profaned among them. 27Her princes in the midst thereof are like wolves ravening the prey, to shed blood, and to destroy souls, to get dishonest gain. The young man that was dancing with the wolves is me! Thankfully, I have recovered and I want to see the body of Christ's discernment sharper than ever so we can see the wolves in sheep clothing exposed and their works dismantled.

2 Corinthians 11:12-15 NIV "And I will keep doing what I am doing in order to cut the ground from under those who want an opportunity to be considered equal with us in the things they boast about. For such people are false apostles,

deceitful workers, masquerading as apostles of Christ. And no wonder, for Satan himself masquerades as an angel of light. It is not surprising, then, if his servants also masquerade as servants of righteousness. Their end will be what their actions deserve." The enemy has released counterfeits that have taken on a religious mindset to try to affect the sheep of God. Some are knowingly being guided by Satan while others are flowing and hurting the sheep unknowingly. Spiritual abuse is something that is very prevalent in the body of Christ. Spiritual abuse is, of course, something that people don't expect to encounter because a pastor or spiritual leader is supposed to be there to love and build them, not turn and tear them down because of their own motives for personal gain. Today, we see so many wolves fooling the people of God to believe that they are a great vessel of God. Spiritual abuse to me is just religious enslavement than anything. Spiritual abuse, in my personal life, dealt with strong intimidation by my leaders, control, and manipulation. Anytime I went outside of what my leaders demanded; I was deemed rebellious and disobedient. It caused such a terrible after effect that I began to be afraid of spiritual leadership.

Wolves are preying on those that are in vulnerable places and will have them doing anything they desire all in the name of their religion and their god. We must be very discerning of these perpetrators. I truly believe anyone that can hurt innocent people and still play church has psychological issues and are affecting the very blueprint of the kingdom that Jesus laid. There are roots that cause a person to lead by intimidation and take away a person's free will. This is not just unrighteous, but this is straight up witchcraft. One of the ways that we see that people are being taken advantage of is through tainting the very essence of spiritual parenting. Leaders are taking their position as parents as a position to control a person's every move and then end up committing spiritual incest by sleeping with their spiritual sons and daughters or those that they mentor. You may be sitting there with your mouth wide open, but it is happening behind the scenes of some of our favorite churches and by our favorite pastor personalities. Even though it is happening in some of the churches, I will be the first to say it is not happening in all. Beware of the wolves that are misusing their authority, seem more angry than joyful, and are greedy for your submission and even your gifts. Wolves that are so perverted and skipped the holiness teachings in Sunday school. These wolves will always look for you to be loyal to them, and honor their authority. Be careful of that leader that wants to control your life and call it to order when they cannot even get their own life in order. Beware of the wolves. I pray my story will keep you from falling into some of the traps I fell into, or if you are under a wolf you will find something that you read in this book that will be your key to freedom. Each chapter will end with a prophetic decree. I would ask that you declare these decrees. Life and death is in the power of our tongues. Just imagine what we can accomplish if we all decree together.

Prophetic Decree: ***I declare and decree that I am reading this book with an open mind and spirit to better understand spiritual abuse, its effects, and what I can do to model the kingdom in the midst of it all. I declare I am a conduit of change along with my brothers and sisters that are reading as well. As spiritual abuse is being exposed, I declare there will be a balance of confronting and solutions to what so many people have experienced.***

Chapter One

Spirit of Rejection

Dear Spirit of Rejection,

I never knew how much of a grip you had on me until the Holy Spirit showed me after I received true deliverance. Rejection, if truth be told, my life has been a roller coaster and I believe I have a mandate to expose you and your powers so that others will not experience what I have been through and if they have I want to make sure they experience true freedom. You caused me to experience your hold as I grew up without a father in my life. My parents had me young and my father did nothing to invest in me as a young boy to adulthood. Because of the lack of love I felt, you were unyielding, rejection. I experienced suicidal thoughts and even attempted suicide on several occasions. You tried me, but you were unable to kill me. O' Spirit of rejection, understand, I followed what I heard many people say and I dedicated my life to that of service in the church. Little did I know that some experiences within in the church would almost be the death of me.

I started preaching at 15, an innocent, young boy that hadn't experienced anything. Nothing could shake me, break me, or steer me wrong, so I thought. As I became more active in the church, I linked up with the wrong crowd. The crowd wasn't the gang on the corner or the drug dealers. The gang I hooked up with was what I call "fake church folk." They look like church, preach like church, shout like church, but if you get too close to them, you realize that they are no church but perpetrators and frauds. I believe they meant well but were guided by the lust of their flesh and by the devil himself. They probably dealt with you (Rejection) and were vulnerable for attention just like me. As I connected to these fake church folk, I began to take on characteristics and traits that I always said that I would never take on.

I remember hearing about leaders that were living undercover lives. They could preach you under the pews and lead you to the sheets of their bed all at the same time, but I always said that would never happen to me. I am strong; I am anointed and nothing can sway me. Well, what happens when you have a broken little boy that was attempting to lead but never came to a place of true deliverance? This broken little boy was targeted by the devil to make a lie out of God. Anointed, destined, but would soon go through the craziest years of his life.

I accepted an identity that God did not create or intend for me. Like the other preachers that I knew were living secret lives, I became that same type of preacher. I would preach the people crazy but would be living a raggedy life. Hey, if no one knew, why tell them. I also began to notice as they would say birds of a feather would flock together. There was no way I could have been around homosexuality and not eventually fall into it. So, I begin to hang out with preachers that were living double lives, but that wasn't the fullness. I began to realize that what I was doing was a major part of the organization I was in. Almost every leader that was in the organization was living a secret life, married but had a side piece. This was perversion at its best. If Jesus had come back, he would have caught a whole bunch of people with their pants down. I noticed that it became pleasure over the Holy Spirit's conviction even for me. I even found myself about to settle into a lifestyle whether God was for it or not. Rejection, you introduced me to your brother named perversion.

My life was not just about perversion, but also the prostitution of my spiritual gifts, loss of my true identity, being manipulated and controlled by spiritual authority. Have you ever been in a place of shame and rejection that you felt that the best thing to do is to stay connected to the people that would harm you more than help you? Even with knowing that my fellowship was a tainted one, I stayed apart for years. Why? It was because of my own insecurities. Yes, I was messed up inside, but they accepted me messed up and at the same time they allowed me to preach and showcase my gifting. I knew I had a strong future, but I felt that it was ok to live wild as long as my leaders accepted me the way I was and wouldn't take ministry from me until I began to be convicted. I remember going to my leader at the time and telling them everything about what I was doing, even my sexual desires for men. The scary thing was they said, "I know, Harold, and what if God never delivers you." My point of going to my leaders, at that time, was for them to walk me through deliverance not just from the perversion but also from your grip, Rejection. This is where I feel that my gifts were prostituted. You have a leader in your church that is so messed up and broken inside that you rather they continue to preach jacked up instead of being made free so that they could minister effectively. Leaders, you do more of an injustice to your leaders by allowing them to practice their gifts while practicing their sins. Godly rebuke and Godly love is what they need. If you love them, you must correct them. So, I was led by my leaders and preached everywhere. Not realizing that the words that I was preaching may have been good to those that like whooping and hollering with the Hammond B3 Organ humming behind them, but I didn't have the ability to set captives free because I wasn't free. I sounded effective but truthfully what I was ministering was ineffective. And I found myself preaching hard against the things that I was doing. I was preaching against sexual sins, perversion, and homosexuality. So not only was I ineffective but I was also a hypocrite. You may ask, why I would preach against something that I was doing. The answer is easy; preach against it, so people don't know you are in it. Let the truth be told, leaders, eventually you will be exposed.

I begin to notice that I was being held captive not only by sins but by the company that I kept. I found myself trying to win people's acceptance, so I became a spiritual slave to my leaders. Whatever they said, I would do. Whatever I saw them doing whether right or wrong, I began to model it. Why? I wanted to be important. I remember trying to get their validation so much. I began to model what I saw in the other leaders. I began to do whatever possible to be recognized in the church and win positions. I was more concerned with the leaders giving me platforms and opportunities than I was about God giving them to me. I watched other people compete for the Bishop's blessings, and opportunities and I became a man pleaser rather than a God pleaser as well. I watched people be elevated to eldership and even Bishops in the church when I knew these were the same people that I hung out with the night before doing ungodly things. But again, I wanted to fit in. I wanted to be deemed important. But I would leave convocations, church services, and church meetings emptier than when I came in. This was because my passion for ministry began to shift to my passion for attention. Everything that I saw I became. Rather than questioning the behavior, I took on the same behaviors and mindsets. I was in need of true deliverance in which I thought I would never get.

Spirit of Rejection

Many will be made free because I refuse to keep silent about our relationship. I am bold enough to say you no longer have a hold on me. God has given me the authority and power to defeat you and your powers. Thanks be unto God I am free.

Signed "He whom the Son has set free."

P.S. I do not blame my behaviors on the church. Again this all stemmed from low self -esteem, rejection, and lack of love for me. But, the origin of my backslidden state was the "church." I understand that you may be someone that is reading my book and at your wits end at what you have seen in the church. And, you want to be one that experiences personal deliverance so that you can be a vessel of deliverance for your generation and for generations to come. One thing the church lacks is true deliverance. I am not referring to emotional services where it looks like deliverance, but people leave the same way. A new wave of deliverance is being released, and it is dependent on the church tapping into transparency that these issues are real and that there have to be some conduits ready to release the Glory of God for true manifestation of healing and deliverance. Are you currently in sin but need deliverance? Do you feel that your leadership is aware of your sin but has turned blinded eyes to it because they see you're gifted and are more concerned with that? Or truthfully, are you one that knows that you have a major calling, but sin has crippled your progress because of the spirit of rejection? This book is definitely for you. Keep reading forward.

You may ask why I started my book addressing the ruthless spirit of rejection. Let me give you a background on my childhood. I was born out of wedlock to my 19-year-old father and 17-year-old mother. I believe that the effects of being an unexpected child to young parents are what created an opportunity for me to deal with rejection. My parents most likely were excited about having a child but time would eventually set in. I began to experience withdraw from my father. I do not believe that it was set in his heart to reject me, but my perception as a young child was that I was being rejected, overlooked, and not loved by him. Who would expect a 19-year-old still finding his identity, to be able to validate the identity of a child? So, this is not to shame him or attack. I love him dearly, but this is to show the effects of the grip of rejection from one that is supposed to fill you. I have read the book "Double Honor" by Dr. Melodye Hilton. I love how she says, "In the natural, you could pour, and pour and pour water over an upside-down cup, but the cup can never be filled because of its position." Just think of that upside down cup being a person that has been rejected. The person knows they are supposed to be filled and they long to be filled but rejection has knocked them upside down, and they cannot be a vessel to be filled. Their posture/position has changed. Remember, their identity requires them to be filled and that is what they were designed for. So, I was that upside down cup. As a young child and even into my teenage years, I was looking for some filling of a void. A male figure, in my life, is what I needed. The need was the driving force that ran me right into the pack of wolves. Here are some proven facts about rejection that I can relate to that I found in an article on rejection at goodtherapy.org. Rejection can be extremely painful because it may have the effect of making people feel as if they are not wanted, valued, or accepted. Children who feel consistently rejected by their parents may find it difficult to succeed at school and in relationships with their peers. Rejection might often contribute to pre-existing conditions such as stress, anxiety, and depression or lead to their development. According to research, the same brain pathways that are activated by physical pain are also activated by social pain or rejection. Receptor systems in the brain also release natural painkillers (opioids) when an individual experiences social pain, the same as when physical pain is experienced. As I came into my teenage years, I tried everything from sex, drugs, and alcohol to fill the voids. I was always quiet and to myself but always would sneak to try something that could fill the voids I had in my life. My God how it would hurt to think that my parent didn't love me.

As I experienced this void in my life, I became extremely needy. Dr. Melodye says in Double Honor, "Our circumstances distort our perception, which is dictating to us how we see ourselves positioned. Our mind and emotions cry out, "I am needy!" With the mentality of "I am needy," we find God pouring out, but it's not saturating us, and we remain passively inactive and empty." Wow, Dr. Melodye is describing my life. I can truly relate to this and the many people reading this can also relate to the feeling of emptiness and neediness. The needy mentality is something that I took on. As I grew up, I always sought and looked for something to fill the emptiness. I was always quiet and stayed to myself. I always looked out the window just waiting for my daddy to return but he never did. So at this point, I needed something to fill me. So, I built a strong relationship with the Lord. To the place that even sometimes my family didn't understand my hunger and thirst after the Lord. At times, I felt filled but at times I still filled empty.

With the needy mentality, I looked to the church to fill the void. I longed for a safe place where I could have my gifts further developed and a place where I felt loved and where I belonged. I began to attend a church, as I stated earlier in this chapter. This church was the perfect place. The leader was very charismatic and preached what I felt was my DNA. The church welcomed me in with welcome arms. The powerful, preached word and worship is what first got my attention. They knew how to go into the presence of God and invoke the sweet Holy Spirit. So, I joined the perfect church as a teenager. At this time, I was already a minister, but the church I attended couldn't fill the voids. They were very traditional and didn't teach on the gifts of the spirit or operate in a prophetic and apostolic flow, in which I knew was in me. So, I joined my new church. It was incredible. Of course, I quickly got into the flow and also was placed on the Ministerial staff. At this time, I started to fill the void filling up. About six months went by, and I was promoting this church to everyone I knew. It was the best place to be for everyone. I helped fill the church up week after week. Carpooling people from my hometown to where the church was located. As time progressed, things began to get a little weird. First I noticed the minister of music was a little too sweet for my taste. You know he was a little sugary. He was very flamboyant. He would play the organ but just had a weird vibe about him. I overlooked it because again, it was the perfect place for me to be. Then, I remember a youth at the church saying that minister of music was being inappropriate with him. He would have the boy come over to his house, and he would massage the boy and rub his hair, etc. He was young and vulnerable, and at first, he didn't think anything was wrong with it but as time progressed he felt uncomfortable. Honestly, I am not sure what else happened as of course, the young man was uncomfortable to tell it all. This was told to the senior leadership, but they overlooked it. This should have been my first sign that I might just be in a den with wolves and didn't know it. I just moved forward. As time progressed, I noticed that the church had all type of leaders in the pulpit. My eyes began to be opened. I saw ministry leaders whose marriages were on the rocks. I saw deacons with drinking problems because you could smell the alcohol on their breath as they would hug you and say "Praise the Lord," and elders with anger problems, etc. Not saying that they had to be perfect, but as Disciples of Christ, they should have been showing a little more Jesus than what they were displaying. God always gives opportunities for escape, but I started settling for things that I would not have settled for before. Maybe my heart couldn't take rejection any longer and didn't want to feel the emptiness. As time progressed, I noticed the senior leader always had a way of covering up the sins that had penetrated the Leadership staff. I wonder if maybe because they were big tithers, or because he valued their friendship over their freedom. Not to mention that the ones that it was evident that they were struggling with sin were being promoted to different positions in the church.

One area that I started noticing more and more was a homosexual spirit and a strong one at that. I began to interact more with the network of churches under our senior bishop. Some that I believe were trying to be discreet but as soon as they opened their mouths to speak their mannerisms confirmed that they were also struggling with this spirit. So, I just saw a den of wolves on a larger scale, from the pulpit to the door. Young men and old men, even some of the young women were in this same strong struggle. This is something that I never wanted to be a part of. How in the world was the Senior Bishop and Bishops board ok with this? Could it be that they were ok with it because they also were in the same stuff?

There was no way that I could be so close to this stuff and not make its move and try to grip me also. Let me tell you about the national youth leader that I came in contact with. Or should I say, I came face to face with a wolf and fell prey to him? I remember that evening that shaped my world and a false identity of me. This was a young man I had seen here and there at some of the regional gatherings and he was very active in the organization. I ran into him at an event, and he asked for my number so we could connect for church purposes. I remember he came to a youth service that I preached at for my church and he seemed pretty cool. So, because I was active in my church and the youth and he was active as well in the same, he had invited me to stay at this house one night before a youth meeting. I took him up on the offer. Why not connect with a young man who was on fire for the Lord, and was making a major impact on his church and youth just like I was? I went over, met his parents, and we hung out that evening. You could tell that he was the apple of his parents' eye and he could do no wrong. The night grew late, and I was getting tired and knew I had to go to bed soon because we had to get to the meeting early and it was about an hour and a half drive. This next part is no joke and is for mature audiences only. And for the first time, I am openly sharing with the world what took place. That evening, he got up and put on a porno as we sat in his basement. I was young and a boy so why not watch a porno with a friend? As we watched, you could tell we both were aroused. He stood up right in front of me and exposed himself to me. I didn't know what to think or say; of course, I was embarrassed, confused, etc. Especially because this young man had gained the respect of so many people in the network and unlike the others that struggled with the homosexuality spirit he wasn't flamboyant nor did he have certain mannerisms. So, I never thought for once that he was attracted to men, let alone me. He proceeded to pull my pants down, and he laid on top of me. First, understand because of how confused I was, I never had a chance to say stop. I never tried to push him off of me. I just let him do whatever he wanted until he released. Once the release happened, he got off of me, and I just laid there like what the heck just happened. Then I got myself together enough to put my clothes back on. He fell asleep, and I just laid there staring at the ceiling. Shame immediately fell on me. Then, I thought maybe this was love. I didn't know. I eventually fell asleep. We woke up the next day, and he could see the confusion on my face, and he just asked are you ok? I said yes, and I rode for that hour and a half to the meeting and back quiet. He tried to make small talk, but I was so confused. He even proceeded to hold my hand, as a sign of safety as we rode back down the road from the meeting. As time progressed, we grew closer and had an on and off relationship for a few years. Mainly because of insecurities on both of our part we had more issues than anything. That needy mentality caused me to look for my void to be filled by this man. Most likely I had this void for the love and attention from a man because of the rejection I had experienced for almost all of my life by my father. To this day, I wonder what type of void he had in his life that caused him to be bold enough to try that with me. Even more importantly, I pray that others have not been taken advantage of by this young wolf.

The voids took me to what I thought was the perfect church and to the perfect friend. I stayed at the church for almost five years and stayed "friends" with him for almost that duration. Neither was good for me; I was dealing with wolves on a daily basis. My identity was distorted and my mind was in a very dangerous place. Sin and perversion will distort one's identity, purpose, and destiny. You can be called into the nations and even travel to the nations, but if you are in sin, you are a counterfeit. You are a counterfeit until you receive authentic deliverance. I became a counterfeit because I allowed my desires to have me in a continual dance with wolves. I would dance around the obvious, dance around my personal shortcomings until wrong no longer felt wrong. I was in a place where wrong felt normal. It felt normal to live two lives and to even experience hurt from the homosexual relationship. It was even to the point where I became numb to physical abuse that I experienced at the hands of him when he became threatened by the attention I would get from other young men that clearly were interested in me. I remember when I was tired of living a double life being the powerful preacher in the pulpit and perverted and broken outside the church. I went to my pastor and said I am tired of living like this; I don't want to be like this anymore. Hoping and praying that he would have strategies for me to get delivered. His response still rings clear in my ear as if he just said it to me today. His response was simply, "Well, what if He doesn't deliver you?" I took that as just accept where you are and what you are doing. Your deliverance is not a guarantee. I knew straight up that a loving God did not desire me to stay in the situation I was in. I guess this is why a lot of people under his leadership are still the way they always were with no deliverance even to this day. This church I believe still has a great purpose and the people in the struggles also have a great purpose, but until they bow to God, they will stay in the same place. Maybe you know a church like this, or maybe you have been in a similar position. I just want to encourage you don't settle for anything that is not God's best for you. Deliverance is always available to those that want it.

Prophetic Declaration: ***I decree and declare that there is a remnant of people that have survived the grip of rejection and are experiencing the true freedom of the Holy Spirit and others that are on the verge of their breakthrough. The spirit that has tried to swallow up their destiny is cut off and the people of God have the victory over it. I decree that the spirit that causes the people of God to walk in fear of rejection is being cast out and the people shall recognize how the Lord and his people view them. Perfect love casts out fear and rejection.***

Chapter Two

Control Freaks!

Every organization experiences control by leadership, sadly even the church. The major motivation of an abusive leader is fear. They lead with the fear that if they are not fully involved or in charge of everything from the affairs of the church to the lives of the people, then they aren't doing their job. This is a false perception to have. They lead by intimidation and often will try to take the place of God in the life of their followers. Religious leaders use their spiritual authority in an ungodly way to manipulate & control their followers.

A religious and abusive leader's main focus is to see what they can gain rather than what they can give and impart into their spiritual recipients. This totally contradicts the model that God has put on true loving leaders. True leaders that are motivated by God's love look to invest, support and groom their spiritual children. They want to see them successful in their calling and to be a positive impact in the world. They don't want anything from their followers but a teachable spirit; open to Godly rebuke motivated by love, and their commitment to do all that God wants them to do. We must ask ourselves "what type of leader am I connected to? And what type of leader am I? Does our leader remind us often that they are the only ones that can hear from God, and if we need to hear from God that God only speaks to them first for us? If so we need to disconnect fast. Does your leader put more emphasis on you honoring them more than you honoring God?

Controlling leaders often expect their followers to come to them first before making life decisions. This can be a major curse in a marriage when a man or woman goes to their leader before going to their spouse to discuss any decisions that need to be made. I have seen this on many occasions where even leaders have encouraged a member of their ministry to leave their spouse if the spouse didn't agree with what the leader said was the right move for the individual. This is not the character of God.

Have you experienced control where your leader tells you how, when, where, and even if you can use your gift? I have personally seen and experienced this, especially when they are threatened by your gift. Or many control your use of your gift because they feel that it is because of them that you are so gifted.

I remember being under a particular leader that I sensed something wasn't right. What I sensed was that she was having an affair with her assistant/armor bearer who was also a female. My spirit would not let it rest. So, I reached out to her to talk about it and she ignored my calls and text messages. I then reached out to the other senior leaders in the organization to get their thoughts and so we could pray. Word got back to the "Apostle," and I was quickly reprimanded. I also held a position as one of her assistants in the organization. But because I went to other leaders, she felt that I broke all trust and I was sat down from my position. A year or so later the things that I felt were confirmed and were brought to light. Her secret life caused her husband to request a divorce. Understand that anyone that is a controlling leader feels they are above Godly rebuke and will punish you for calling them out on their mess. I remember being reminded by that leader that I was out of line for bringing my concerns up and that I would be cursed for not trusting her as my leader. I 100% respected her, but respect doesn't say you cannot in Godly love question or challenge them. It is funny, because they always wanted me to release the word of the Lord over their lives until the word of the Lord revealed their secret sin. Also, understand that I was very familiar with the homosexual spirit so it could not be hidden from me no matter who it was dealing with it.

What do you do when you believe you are following the voice of God but your leader reminds you again that you are to hear God through them? God has put the ability in each of us to hear His voice. This does not mean we do not take heed to the voice of seasoned leaders with the voice of wisdom. But many people are listening to the lies of leaders that cannot hear God themselves but always have a word for others. It is such a threat to religious leaders when you can hear God for yourself. First, because you will be able to discern their wrong motives and disconnect, and secondly because you will not be driven by them but by the Holy Spirit. I remember I followed the voice of God when he told me to disconnect from my previous leaders, their church, and the organization. Understand that I was rejected at that point, and I was known as a renegade. I have heard this so many times that "Rejection is God's protection." Those wolves did me a favor by not speaking to me and nonchalantly pushing me out of their circle. It took about seven years for me to understand that nothing about that ministry and those leaders were good for me. I say that the rejection was God's protection because if I would have stayed, I honestly believe I would have experienced either spiritual or even natural death. There was so much confusion and contradiction to the word. To this day the same thing is happening. Being under that type of leadership reminds me of Matthew 23:4 where Jesus himself is speaking: "Indeed religious leaders crush you with impossible demands and never lift a hand to help ease the burden." They crush and push you into a mode that you were not originally designed for. Their mode/model is so perverted that your personal identity is lost so that you can look like, act like, preach like, shout like them, all while living a sin filled life. There becomes such a burden on you that you don't know what to do and they don't lift a finger to assist you. They just tell you to praise your way through, dance, shout, etc.,

Being under a controlling leader puts a false sense of responsibility on you that makes you feel like you need to perform, and conform to their religious systems to gain their acceptance. As one that was rejected, I was always looking for the acceptance of my spiritual leaders even if I knew their systems contradicted God's way. The result is Matthew 9:36 where you do all of this to get their attention and acceptance and still feel bewildered without a leader. You work so hard trying to get acceptance that you have a bigger void than when you started. You begin to strive for their attention. I remember how everyone reminded me that I was the apple of my Bishops' eye and how hurt and disappointed he was when I left out of the church. The reality was I was serving Him more than I was serving God.

There is such a misuse of Spiritual authority today. The dynamic is so bad that we literally have controlling leaders becoming more of slave-owners then Heaven Ambassadors. We have church leaders today that are slave-owners while their membership has become their slaves. I remember feeling more like a spiritual prostitute that would perform for the church while the pimp (my spiritual leader) sat back and reaped the benefits.
When one is infatuated with the gifts of their "spiritual children" they push for them to perform even if they aren't fully developed and ready. I experienced this as a young minister. I could move a crowd, fill a church, and was well-known for preaching them under the pews. I was

elevated to Eldership at the age of 16. Now, what 16-year-old truly knows how to lead in the capacity of an elder? The people saw the gift and even my future but overlooked the reality that I was still immature and needed development not to mention, deliverance.

I believe, with all my heart, that the Body of Christ is being rescued. But, we must be open to receive God's re-direction. Many will find themselves discerning things that may not be right and God may instruct you to leave. And in this, you must be bold enough to stand against all the wiles of the enemy because if you are under a controlling leader, he or she will do their best to keep you in their church, under their covering, and bound. They will instill fear in you that if you try to leave that you will be cursed, and the blessings of God cannot be received. Many people are sitting in the same church that God told them to leave years ago because their leader has put so much fear in them. Don't waste any more time if you sense it, seek counsel, and quickly shift.

Jesus never motivated the body of Christ through fear. Fear is derived from control and is a form of manipulation which is a sin. Instead of motivating people through love and encouraging the people of God to walk out their purpose set by God they motivate through manipulation, controlling every move of the believer. With discernment, the people of God will realize that they aren't going in the direction of God but the direction of that leader.

I was at my wit's end, when it came to my last controlling leader. He was trying to control me and control everything that I did in the church that my wife and I birthed even before coming under his covering. He made me teach from his elder's manual and ordain leaders the same way that he did. Anything that was outside the way that he did something was out of order or not of God. Anytime I would begin to shift and go in a direction that he wasn't used to, he would quickly rebuke me and tell me to be humble and not to go outside of what he as my "Chief Apostle" was teaching me. It became crazy. I was at my last straw with him when my church had planned an outreach initiative in our community. This just so happened to fall on the same day as an ordination service that he wanted me to be a part of. He told me I must cancel the event and come to the ordination. There was a lot of planning, money, and time invested in our outreach initiative. So I, of course, prayed on which direction I should go in. I even reached out to him and told him that I couldn't make his event. When I did this, he became so angry. I could not believe how furious he was. I was looking for him to tell me that I was very mature and kingdom-minded for wanting to be out in my community making a difference, but what I desired did not happen. He started to blow up my phone with threatening texts and calls, saying he was going to revoke my ordination and that I would be cursed. It was very concerning when he came out and said that if I didn't do what he said that my wife and I would die. He said it would be an Ananias and Sapphira experience. At that point, I quickly went to my wife and said even if we have to be uncovered for a while; we needed to end our relationship with this Apostle. Before I could even reach back out to him, he sent word that he was making my apostleship null and void. Now, please remember that man can't make or strip someone of their apostleship or any five-fold ministry calling. This is from God. He even had one of his friends, who was in ministry call me on three way with him to try to mediate the situation. It started ok, but it quickly shifted to his friend also telling me that I need to obey my leader and that if I didn't my ministry would not prosper. He even went on to say that Apostle held the key to my destiny and that I would be cursed if I didn't straighten up and listen to him. At the end of the call, I advised them both that we will be going forward with our event. So, we went on with the event and people were blessed. We had seen people come to Christ; the homeless received a hot meal, struggling families received medical assistance and clothing. We also had some of the most anointed singing groups come and render music during the event. It was the best thing that could have ever happened to our community. I believe it was only a day or so from the event that I started receiving texts and calls from people connected to him advising how wrong I was and that we should have been at the ordination service. We quickly sent back everything that belonged to him specifically the documents that were produced and signed by him and the other apostles at my affirmation/commissioning service. Even though I never saw it, I understand that he wrote an email to a lot of the leaders that we were mutually connected to, to advise that I was rebellious and that he would no longer cover me. He also attempted to bring shame and a bad reputation to my name and my ministry. See what measures a control freak will go to attempt to control you. He thought that I would still be controlled by his hands by attempting to humiliate me and close doors and opportunities for me. I understand now more than ever that a wolf does not want their followers to make judgments on their own, And because of fear, the sheep are victims of control. "Allowing fear to dominate hinders your ability to solve simple problems while internal peace releases creative solutions." Dr. Melodye Hilton. If you are controlled, you will never be able to make sound judgments or make the necessary moves in your life, because you will always look for your leader to tell you what to do next.

Coming out from under a controlling leader did not keep me from being one myself. I can go back and see now. I wish I would have seen it while I was doing it that I was just as bad as the leaders I was under. I was very demanding, often rude, and had to have my hands in everything. I would put people in positions but still would control every move that they made, saying I am the pastor I need to be involved so that nothing would go wrong. I even got involved in the personal lives of those under my leadership. Even though I considered them spiritual children, I was taking on the mindset that they were actually of a child's age.

Another aspect of control that I had to come to a realization about was the slave mentality. I remember learning about the incredible progress since the slavery movement. We have seen and learned of the horrific experiences that the black slaves endured at the hands of their slave owners. What if I told you the same Spirit that manifested in slavery time is still manifesting today in some of our local assemblies?

The slave owners used religion to keep African Americans subservient to them to make them feel that slavery was Gods way to keep them as servants, and if they stayed slaves, God would reward them one day. This, unfortunately, has carried into the African American Churches of today. But instead of a white slaveholder, they have a Spiritual leader that controls their every move, decision, and even life. This spirit of slavery has caused many believers to accept being controlled by their leader, and at times they don't even see it as control. They have been brainwashed to believe this is how a leader is supposed to treat their followers. I am here to dispel that myth. It is sad to say that some leaders that are preaching to us weekly at times can be viewed as "Master" and what they say goes. I fully believe in honor and Godly submission to your leaders, but I also believe that if the wrong person gets a hold of authority, they can use it to use and abuse people.

In the 1770's, many black slaves converted to evangelical religions. But, many of the slave owners and preachers preached strict obedience to the slave owners rather to God. The slaves were required to attend only the services held by slave master because they felt that if they allowed them to go to other churches that they would plot rebellion against their owners. Again, this is in direct correlation of what is happening in the lives of innocent brainwashed members. They are under serious domineering leaders that do not allow their membership to go to other churches or conferences because they know if they get out they will find that what they are being taught and how they are being treated would cause them to seek freedom and leave.

As time progressed, some slave owners allowed their slaves to have open religious meetings among themselves. As some freely worshiped on Sundays only, some slaves were forbidden to as some slave-owners did not believe that "Negroes" had souls, so they didn't need religion. To better understand the control we must understand the whys. What does control by leaders in the church especially in the African American church have to do with slavery? The connection was when the slaves began to start their own church gatherings; this was the only time they were allowed to carry titles, form their government, and be in charge. Sound familiar. So, this spirit has manifested today in the lives of leaders because the only time they had authority they believe is if they held a position in the church and from there they pervert their leadership role and misuse their followers. They were only important in their own eyes when they were in church on Sunday leading. This speaks volumes. It could also explain why we have so many Sunday Christians. They only feel empowered to lead and serve in the body of Christ on Sundays only.

My wife and I were under this type of control. We had a leader that first called himself a "Chief" Apostle. We could see after time that they used terms like "Chief Apostle" or "Master Prophet" due to his hunger and drive for control. Often, I was advised that I was not allowed to consult or receive from other Apostles or Prophets concerning my ministry. Why? This was because like the slave owner he felt that we were his property and he didn't want us to get to our freedom. This was manipulation at its best. And like many others, I stayed connected to this leader and believed his lies. Again, I wasn't his spiritual son, but he viewed me as his property.

The slave owner and my "Chief Apostle" was the same person. Many people asked me why I stayed under that type of leader and I realized this was a generational struggle. I accepted being treated this way because that was the way of my ancestors. I needed true deliverance. I saw this person as anointed so I didn't want to buck against him because I was reminded many times by him that he was my apostle and that I would do what he said. But, truth be told he wasn't truly anointed. He was a WOLF in disguise. I have heard many times how the African American people have celebrated that they have escaped the man or have been delivered from the grips of slavery. But the true testament is they have not escaped the man and the slave mentality, and they need to look at who they submit themselves to as their Godly leader. They are being bound with chains of manipulation and control and are being beaten with the whips of deception.

I have watched behind closed doors how leaders that have "rule over God's people" can truly be. You have some that are truly God sent and God led and would never treat a person in a negative way. Then, I have seen people more so of my race treat people like they are their subordinates or worst yet that they are 2-year-olds and if they do something wrong they will be put in time out. This is not the model that we should accept in our churches. When Jesus dealt with his disciples, he treated them as grown men, not as children. Many people have taken the term of Spiritual Parenting to another dimension. This has become so bad that a person under this type of slave master leadership cannot make their own choices unless they first run it past their leader.

Are you currently under this type of leadership? Let me tell you the effects of being under this type of leadership. I can only speak from my personal experience. When under this type of leadership, you begin not to be able to discern the voice of God for yourself. This can be very dangerous. God could be telling you something that could save your life but because the voice of God has become so dim because you only know the voice of your leader you could end up in a dangerous place. Even more serious, you could find yourself outside the will of God. I could remember many times sharing with my leader what I felt God was saying to me concerning the direction of my ministry, but he would always shut it down and say that is not God, but God is saying this instead. So, I was under the impression that God was no longer speaking to me and that I had to always depend on my leader for direction. I lost confidence in my calling and my discernment. If you are under this type of leader, they are operating in witchcraft. A true leader will always encourage their followers or spiritual children to discern the voice of God for their selves. Never allow a man's voice to replace or override God's voice. When I linked up with my true spiritual parents, I was always afraid to express what I felt God was saying with the fear of being shot down or rejected. Thankfully my leaders were able to discern where I came from and encouraged me in everything that God was speaking for me to do.

Prophetic Declaration: ***I decree and declare that the true motives of the leaders within the body of Christ will be seen. These motives will be motives of the King that will advance his kingdom on the earth. Anything contradictory to the nature of God is coming to an end. Selfless leaders are arising so that the depiction of heaven can be viewed and experienced on the earth. I decree that I am a leader that this world has been looking for. I am a part of God's great army.***

Chapter Three

Religious Spirit

Anytime you deal with an unrighteous leader in the church today, they are normally comprised of these attributes: pride, perversion, performance and they are platform/position driven. These attributes or characteristics can be identified as one with a religious spirit. A leader with a religious spirit will not demonstrate the fruits of the Spirit that Paul speaks of in Galatians 5:22-23. If you don't see these attributes, then you are dealing with a toxic and dangerous wolf.

Pretense- When dealing with religious leaders I always noticed that they wear masks. What you see may be what you get, but it is not who they really are. They pretend like their marriage is great when the reality is it is just a ticking bomb ready to explode. In the eyes of the audience, they always seem like they have it together and they are strong, but the reality is they are only moments away from a nervous breakdown. And you dare not go to them for wisdom about the condition of your heart or what you are struggling with secretly because they will teach you how to suppress your issue rather than addressing your issue. With this pretense, I took on this thing. I was hurting, disgusted, and wanted freedom but I didn't know how to get it so I would dance around my issues with the rest of the wolves and abused in my church. I was truly dancing with wolves and didn't know if the music would ever stop. Wolves have been motivated by the enemy to pretend like they are sent by God to get the attention of the saints and to lead them away from their destiny instead of to their destiny. Proverbs 14:12 KJV: "There is a way which seemeth right unto a man, but the end it leads to death." This is why it is so important to try the spirit by the spirit to make sure what you are submitted to is not a perverted fake system. Wolves have a tendency to lack transparency. Again, everything that has to do with them or their life is a pretense. So they share as little as possible.

Pride- I believe pride is so easy for a leader to fall into if they are not careful, because of the celebrity mentality that is placed on them by their followers. From there the emphasis is placed more on them than on Christ as the Savior. Then the leader is driven more by the applause of a man than the approval of God. A leader with this issue is very much self-absorbed to the point where they surround themselves with the "yes" crowd because they hate to be told no to any of their ideas or initiatives. Their core leadership strokes their already prideful spirit by always agreeing. This is why they play favoritism to manipulate the saints to get what they want. And if one person decides to dissent or shares their view that could challenge the leaders, you better get ready for this prideful leader to blow a fuse and have an angry outburst.

A prideful leader has a distorted understanding of respect. They believe that everyone that comes under their leadership automatically should show them respect, instead of believing that respect is earned. I was under leadership that always taught on respecting and honoring them, and the best way was to ensure I was fully submitted to them. There was such an overemphasis where I had to ask if they thought they were God.

When a person has a strong religious and prideful spirit, they feel their voice should be heard louder than anyone or anything else, even to the point where they try to play the voice of God. They are the only one who hears God. One thing that continues to amuse me is when a leader stresses the importance of them covering you or being your covering, but if you ask who their covering is it's a mystery. And along this line, they would advise that they were more of an apostle or covering then almost everyone else. The above are examples of pride and control. If you are experiencing any of this, don't be crazy and say you are waiting for God to tell you to leave, save yourself and leave immediately.

Perversion- This is a topic I speak of throughout the book but wanted to reiterate the danger of perversion in leadership. This is a true sign that someone is just religious and not true to their relationship with God. They are driven by fleshly satisfaction and will do whatever they need to, to ensure they get flesh gratification. As I have shared my own testimony that I came out of a serious lifestyle of homosexuality. The period was over a span of a few years, but I still maintained my status as a minister. I believe I had so much pride in me that I felt like God needed me so he wouldn't take his anointing from me. I had a sense of entitlement. Pride and perversion mixed together is very scary. When you are in both and I noticed this to be true of a lot of the wolves that I encountered, you pick out which sins in your eyes are acceptable. Wolves have a tendency to bend the word to accommodate their lifestyles. Bending the word shows one's lack of reverence to God and obedience to His Word. They bend the word and place a spotlight on everyone else's sin. Perversion and pride cause wolves to be the biggest hypocrites of them all. I have even seen now a greater influx of wolves coming out of the closet and saying that the scriptures against homosexuality was for a specific time, more specifically the Old Testament, and now they are leading churches with their same-sex spouse, saying this is the will of the Lord. We can no longer let the wolves blind us with their religious mindsets. We must speak the truth, live the truth, and walk the truth out.

I also was so bound that I couldn't see myself free or at times didn't want to see myself free. The religious mind would tell me just preach it's just the way things are, or it's just the way God made you. I also saw some of the most anointed men (in my eyes) sleeping around, living double lives, but their perversion didn't stop them. Now as I look over the lives of most of them today versus years ago, they either aren't preaching, or they are preaching but the multitudes of doors that were once open are now closed, some have literally died of AIDs. Success in our eyes is different than God's perception. This is something I had to learn. That one's success is not based on platforms, but it is based on obedience. Today, I live a life of obedience and because of that, I am now on platforms that would most likely eventually fade away because of my lifestyle. Obedience will always defeat perversion.

Another form of perversion that we don't talk about is the leader's view of the people. Often time this is perverted because the leader sees that the people are means to their ends. In other words, they see them as project or a charity case, not as God's people who need mentoring and developing. So these leaders dismiss them before they even attempt to pour into them. Perversion will distort your view of the treasures God has put in your life. With this, I was under a leader who lacked the ability to pour into me. They wanted to call me spiritual son, display me at convocations by allowing me to "preach the house down" but when I would seek them for impartation; they would say things like, "Oh, the Holy Spirit will give you the revelation you need or Harold, you are trying to be too deep." They would dismiss me and my hunger for impartation. So, I often felt misunderstood and lost on what God was saying to me.

This takes me to my next focus which is, ***Performance!***

I often feel that unrighteous leaders specifically wolves put on a grand performance week after week. They preach to get the people hyped when most of the time what they are preaching is not what they are living. Again, they have become entertainers and are not lifting up the Lord to draw people unto Him but to them. When did preachers become performers? They became performers because like me they had a sense or need for acceptance and applause. So, if I want acceptance why not preach what the people want to hear vs. what God wants to say? Who wants to be booed off stage? Despite the reaction of the people in the congregation, we must preach the word of God, we are not to add or take away. When the word of God is preached with sincerity and reverence of heart, there is a heaven performance of true miracles, signs, and wonders. Go by God's script, and He will get the standing ovation.

Wolves have a tendency to hold people hostage from their deliverance. They perform in the pulpit so that people return to their services (show) week after week. They preach these emotionally charged messages to keep people coming back to them for more. It is a method of manipulation. People are being drawn in by the personality of their leaders, but the messages aren't hitting the areas of weakness, hurt, or sin that it needs to hit. If they keep preaching the feel good messages that lead people into a crazed praise break they begin to dance with the wolves, their flesh is stroked, and the issue is never confronted. The result, which is a bad one, is that the people's focus and dependency is now off of God and on man. God is shutting down the one man show, and bringing in a remnant that is not concerned about filling the pews but filling the people with strategies that will help them recognize what authority they possess, what belongs to them, and what God said about them. From this, the sheep will be hungry for truth. The remnant of righteous leaders will follow the words of Paul in 1 Corinthians 2:4 NIV "And my message and my preaching were very plain. Rather than using clever and persuasive speeches, I relied only on the power of the Holy Spirit." Get the actors out of our pulpits, and watch God arise!

The last area that wolves in leadership tend to chase after is ***position.*** Everything they do is to be recognized and promoted to the next big title. They are willing to have a title hooked to their name without the function. One thing that is for sure you would never go to a doctor just because they have Dr. before their name. You go to them because they have been proven, tested, and confirmed as such. You go because they have a good reputation. We have wolves chasing after position and can't even spell Apostle or Prophet. They want to be served rather than serving God's people. Just like with the performance characteristic, they always want to be seen or heard and shine in public. Wolves seek so much power that they neglect their family. The funny thing is they make sure that they put a greater emphasis on their title than their actual name. They find validation in what people call them, rather than what God says about them. You can always tell a power/position hungry wolf because they always speak ill words towards those that are truly functioning in the office that they want. They try to discredit them so that they look better in the eyes of the people. Remember God calls people into certain functions, not man. Man is just called to recognize what God has already said. Psalm 75:6-7 "For promotion *cometh* neither from the east, nor from the west, nor from the south. But God *is* the judge: he putteth down one and setteth up another.

I have recognized that wolves can produce other wolves. I say that because I begin to model what I saw my leaders model. I carried such a spirit of ***pride*** it was crazy. Romans 10:3 says: "For, being ignorant of the righteousness of God, and seeking to establish their own, they did not submit to God's righteousness." I flowed in such self-righteousness that other leaders could not correct me, or give me sound counsel because I was the prophet or the pastor. I believed what they felt was irrelevant. My pride caused me to feel like I was the only one that could speak into the lives of people and see the prophecies come to pass. Not to mention I was the Bishop's spiritual son and armor bearer so you couldn't tell me anything. I am sharing this because it is so important to recognize that unrighteous behavior results in a duplication of unrighteous behaviors. Not to mention all of the ***perversion*** I was in. My pride would get in the way so much that I would be so quick to call out other people's perversion but overlooked my own. Sometimes your own pride and perversion will blind you of your own mess but bring into focus everyone else's problems. **Proverbs 28:13** *People who conceal their sins will not prosper, but if they confess and turn from them, they will receive mercy.* People would even give me words that they saw death on me and sin in my life, but because I was prideful, even those words just went into one ear and out the other. Again, if my leaders wouldn't correct me, why do I care what other people thought or said? I now recognize that this attitude and disregard for holiness and deliverance could have caused me not to be able to write this book. Instead, you could be reading my death notice or obituary. The perversion that was in my life should have had me in a casket buried. But God gave me grace and a second chance to change my life, and to expose the wolves that continue to dance and torment God's sheep. Seeing the ***performance*** of wolves as a young person, I went into this same pattern. Preach until they shout, and make sure they invited me back to do it all over again. The more I preached, and the more doors opened for me, my head began to swell. Not only did my head swell but my perception of my own identity was that I was good for nothing but preaching. I felt my only value was preaching for crowds. As doors began to close, or my itinerary began to slow down, I would beat myself up and allowed myself to think that I was no longer a value to people. I had to learn that preaching wasn't my only gift or purpose. Some people put such an emphasis on their ministry that if you take it away or slow it down, they feel that they were no longer needed for God's purpose. I had a false perception of myself, and I had to find my true identity in Christ. Performance for me pushed me to be ***position*** driven rather than purpose driven. I validated myself based on titles and recognition from man. I can sit back and laugh about it today because I went from Minister, Elder, and then Bishop within just a few years. I know for a fact today that God never called me to be a Bishop. But again, when all you saw was people being promoted year after year based on what they could do for the Senior Leader and not based on what God said, you become distorted in mind and it affects your true ability to function in what God has called you to.

This religious spirit has truly shaped the church into a design that God did not ordain for it to be. The most righteous institute has been molded into one of the most perverted places. What grieves me is to see how we have taken this pride, performance, perversion, and positions to build a structure or I would even be opened to say principality that is all about hierarchy. What I mean is we have such a perverted structure that contradicts what God had in mind. We have where the senior leader is at the top of the pyramid, and the membership is at the bottom, which makes it easy for the 4 P's to be in motion within our church. Any righteous leader will see that the structure is actually the leadership on the bottom to build up and support the membership to reach their highest potential. This will keep us from this religious spirit attempting to control people, when the leaders know their position. We must evaluate how we have structured our leadership in the church. This lack of accountability from our leaders is very unfortunate. Even to the place where these leaders are expecting their followers to display behaviors of holiness that they don't display. They have this "Do as I say, not as I do" syndrome. The religious spirit makes our places of worship look worldlier than the world does itself. We have taken on a mindset that what is perverted is the norm. Sins have become acceptable, and it has become ok to bend the word to accommodate our lifestyles or the lifestyles of our loved ones. The church has lost her flare when abominable acts have become justifiable. This shows a serious lack of reverence to God and His word. I believe that many have shifted into this religious mindset to avoid having to go through the persecution of calling sin what it is, WRONG! In today's society when a minister exercises their right to free speech and their mandate from heaven to preach the unadulterated word, this religious spirit raises its head and its voice, sometimes even louder than the world to say this is a hate speech and that we are to love everyone. I fully agree love should be our motive. Could it be that the love of Christ is attempting to steer someone in the right direction to save their souls, and to bring restoration to their God-given purpose?

One area that the wolves are infiltrating is the very image of the church. I am starting to see more and more in the church, the idea to allow a same-sex couple lead a congregation. That religious spirit deems it ok. And the crazy thing about it is these churches are being packed out. I will never forget when I logged on Facebook and saw a Pastor and his husband. They were called Pastor so-and-so and First Gentlemen-so and-so. What surprised me was that most of the comments on the picture were from church people even some I knew affirming and condoning this. It was the first time I saw it, and as time progressed, it became more accepted and more and more people were coming out that they were openly homosexual and weren't stepping down from ministry. They would be continuing the work of ministry with their new same-sex spouse. The reason I am so passionate about this topic is again, because I was in this and could of went down this same path, deceiving no one but myself, but God brought the proper alignment to me. Just because we affirm something doesn't mean God does. A former friend of mine, discussed with me how he was going to start going to an open affirming church because he was tired of churches coming against the same sex relationships. He went on to say that his dad was a pastor and he had grown up hearing all the lies that God doesn't agree with homosexual relationships. He even went on to tell me that God never spoke against homosexuality in the New Testament, and that the teachings were Old Testament teachings and that we serve a progressive and accepting God. My jaw dropped. How could someone that grew up in a Christian home now say that what people are teaching against sin is not right? Again, this is where we see this religious spirit attempting to take over the church universal ignoring the issues at hand. God loves all people, but he does not love the sin that people participate in. Wolves are being exposed and have an opportunity to go through the proper healing and deliverance like I did. Unfortunately some will be so full of themselves that they won't take heed to the warning to stop affecting the sheep with unrighteous motives.

Prophetic Declaration: ***I decree and declare that the people of God are no longer driven by a religious spirit. Perversion, pride, pretense and the need for promotion/position will no longer operate in our churches or ministries. God is releasing His people to operate in the fruits of the Spirit according to Galatians 5, and anything outside of this is counterfeit, and it will not succeed. I decree that God is routing his people on as we obtain the victory through his son, Christ Jesus.***

Chapter Four

Premature Release

One of the greatest injustices that many wolves in sheep clothing continue to do is to release people into ministry before their time. This is where wolves are using control and manipulation to put people into a position that God has not released them into as of yet. This to me is a Predator and Prey situation. 1 Timothy 5:22 is very clear by saying do not lay hands on any man suddenly. Over these last few years, I have seen such an influx of people being released into ministry because indeed they are gifted and have major potential but no one has taken the time to prove these ministers, train, or impart into them. This has caused a major imbalance in the Kingdom of God causing more chaos then Kingdom Expansion.

As a minister who started preaching at 15, my leaders always would speak of the potential that they saw and I was afforded many opportunities. But, very rarely was the pre-requisite of maturity and the making of the man before the ministry spoken. My leaders were often infatuated by the gifts of the younger leaders and focused mainly on allowing them to display or spotlight their gifts through preaching and prophesying. Ministry cannot be about gifts alone; it has to be about the maturity and integrity of that individual as well. I found myself almost 15 years later having to go back and rebuild the "man" to accommodate the ministry that was built in me. What do you mean? What I am saying is, unrighteous leaders taught on the importance of building a global ministry but never spoke on building my integrity, character, and even having right motives in ministry. I remember being able to preach the house down but lacked in my own personal responsibilities. I was preaching while at the same time my personal life was falling apart. Why? The answer is obvious. I lacked personal conviction and ran from personal responsibilities. I was taught how to take care of the house of God, but not how to take care of my personal affairs. I was living an unbalanced life. More specifically, I remember traveling here and there preaching, and one day the vehicle I was rolling in was repossessed. Why? Again, I was horrible with managing my life. How many preachers do you run into that have jacked up lives but always want to preach to someone? Do you know why this is, because the church has taught us to look the part, but you don't have to be the part? The deep religious side of me would always say, "Why is the devil attacking me again?" I had to wake up, grow up, and realize the enemy was not attacking me. These were self-inflicted struggles. I put these unnecessary pains on myself. Not only were my personal responsibilities not up to par, but I had major struggles within my flesh. As one that was preaching, I lacked major deliverance. As I stated in previous chapters, I dealt with a serious demon of perversion. I had both homosexual and heterosexual perverted relationships. I was sex-crazed. And get this, my leaders were 100% aware. So, I continued in those ways. A righteous leader would say, "Harold, you can't continue like this. You have to get it right." All I had in my heart was just continue to perform on the platforms, and that is all that matters. I came to a very dark place where I didn't care that I had some struggles, as long as I preached like I was free that's all that matter. Eventually, the performing would catch up with me, and I would have a true encounter with the king.

I was driving home from work one evening and had an open vision. Within this vision, the Lord showed me a Neonatal Intensive Care Unit (NICU). Within this NICU the Lord showed me so many babies that were birthed before their time. It was a very hard sight to see, all of these babies were hooked to machines and tubes, because they were released too early. The Lord quickly spoke to me and said, "There are many leaders that were birthed prematurely and are now fighting for their spiritual lives and to be effective in the ministry that I did indeed call them to, but they were released into before I ordained it." The only way of survival for someone that has been released before their time is for them to admit it, and go back and honor the process that God has laid out for them. They must be connected with people that are more so concerned with their natural and spiritual health than their calling and gifting.

If we want to see a true move of God, we must release people into ministry based on the timing of God and the backing of heaven. Just because one is gifted and has a call does not mean they are ready to walk that out as soon as they walk in the door. We must ensure that our ministries develop its membership first in the foundational principles before we release them into ministry. We have a lot of babies trying to walk out what only a mature person can walk out. One of the greatest leaders and apostolic fathers in the word gives us a pre-requisite for leadership in (1 Tim

3). One thing that v.6 says is, "He must not be a ***recent convert*** (convert), or he may become puffed up with conceit and fall into the condemnation of the devil." When placing someone in a position or giving them a title before their time will cause them to walk in arrogance, where they will feel that they have arrived and that no one can tell them anything. They will walk in a lack of humility. A true leader walks with confidence but Godly humility.

You may ask, what is the benefit to wolves to release these people into ministry before their time? I honestly believe that the leaders use it as personal gain for themselves to build their own ministry and platform. The reason I believe it is a personal gain is that often people measure their success based on what can be seen. Meaning if I am releasing many people into ministry it will look like I am successful in the eyes of man. I have seen where churches are filled up because the followers are looking to be the next big name or big preacher and the pastor is known for ordaining and licensing everyone that comes in the door. As I do believe in the raising up and releasing of leaders, I wholeheartedly believe they must be prepared and released after a level of maturity has been reached. And not their gifts alone, but they need to be matured as a man or woman of God. A religious act I see often is where a novice is given a service of ordination. In that service, the novice is dressed in religious garments and presented to the congregation to imply that they are now suited to move forward in ministry. Quite frankly, you can dress up anyone and have a dress up party but all it is, is a costume. You can dress up the outside but if the inside is not clothed in righteousness you are wasting thousands of dollars having grand services and God is not even in it. Another reason a leader will release immature leaders into ministry is because the immature or novice will depend on that senior leader for everything. Some examples are: Hearing the voice of God, discerning the next move that they should take. This is control at its best. You were released into ministry by your leader, but you always have to go to them for major decisions that you have to make, even personal decisions. Again, this is control and manipulation. When a senior leader releases someone before their time and without the backing of heaven, that senior religious leader becomes GOD to the novice. And they can control everything that person does by manipulating them. That novice becomes a puppet and their leader becomes the puppeteer. The immature leader will always be moved by the strings attached by their puppeteer. The puppeteer will also remind the one that they are controlling that if they honor them as their leader they will do what they say and the result will be unmerited favor and blessings. My prayer is that everyone being controlled by a leader will see it and cut the strings. No man or woman is to control another man or woman. This is not biblical and it should not be practiced.

Before releasing anyone into ministry, we must follow the basic biblical principles laid out in the Holy word. The Apostle Peter was very direct concerning one's character and maturity in 2 Peter 1:5-9. If one cannot follow these principles, then they are not cut out for ministry. We have to love our spiritual sons and daughters enough to tell them they still have areas that they need to allow God's power to intervene with. Just because they are gifted does not qualify them. This is why we have so many gifted but perverted preachers in our pulpits. Peter said as Believers we must possess virtue which is positive character traits. He goes on to tell us in v. 8 that these things must be in us and abound. Abound is translated in the Greek as ***pleonzonta*** which means increasing. The Godly character must be forever increasing for one to be qualified to be released into ministry. We should be ever increasing in our maturity and deliverance. From this, we will be able to see that one's fruit is good. The opposite is that one can whoop, holla, preach, prophesy, and pray, cast out devils and all at the same time live unholy in God's eyes they are barren. Barren in the Greek is translated as ***argo*** which means they are unproductive and useless.

There are negative effects of releasing someone into ministry prematurely. I was one that was released into ministry before I obtained maturity and I am going to share with you what the effects were. First, it was hard because I always felt like I had to prove myself and my anointing to people which was a result of insecurity. It always felt like someone was questioning my ability to lead. With this I was often driven by the team of I, then the team of WE. In other words, it was difficult to partner with others to do ministry because I didn't feel anyone was good enough to do ministry with me. This in return, left me alone. A major thing that no one shared with me was that with ministry it would open my life to warfare. When you do not develop one to know how to deal with warfare, especially someone immature they quickly want to throw in the towel and give up. Ministerial relationships were often hindered because I didn't take heed to sound wisdom, thinking I was always right and that people were just trying to stop me from doing the will of the Father because they were jealous of me. If truth be told, they were trying to help me not to make some of the same mistakes that they had made. I was platform and spotlight driven, and I felt the best way to do this was to please others to obtain success. I also felt that the only way of being successful was if I was in the pulpit. That was the only time I felt like I was in my element.

One who is immature often has an issue with submitting to an authority figure. They do not like nor do they feel that being accountable is necessary. It is critical to submit yourself to someone that you can be accountable to that will not tell you what you want to hear but carry a responsibility to tell you what you need to hear. When you have someone that loves you, they will love you enough to tell you about some areas in your life that need to be cleaned up. Hebrews13:17 Obey them that have the rule over you, and submit yourselves: for they watch for your souls, as they that must give account, that they may do it with joy, and not with grief: for that *is* unprofitable for you.

I had a young man that I begin to mentor for ministry. He had a major calling on his life. This calling was the only thing that he was focused on. He was only in his late twenties and had been through multiple wives, kept losing jobs, etc. He had some soul issues. I begin to mentor him more of how to be mature as a man, and then we would focus on maturing him as a Minister. I believed as I have heard Bishop Hamon of Christian International say many times that God makes the man before He makes the ministry. I wanted to see this young man developed in maturity. The young man became offended when I would call out different things that I would discern. He would talk about getting ordained and released into a prophetic ministry. I would always bring him back to reality that, "Sir, there are still something's God wants to work on." Eventually, he didn't want to comply and left the ministry and cut all ties. I later learned that another Pastor ordained him. At first, this hurt me in the natural, but I realized that he was not looking for accountability he was looking for a platform. When we get like this, we lack something very simple. We lack Soul Consciousness. We get so focused on the end result (ministry platform) that we do not take the time to deal with our Soul's infirmities. A spiritual leader sent from God will always remind you to be conscious of the condition of your soul. Many may see this as a demotion, but if you comply, you will receive a major promotion that only comes from God. Immaturity will always say I don't have anything that I need to work on. Maturity will always keep you in a place of soul-consciousness. Don't try to divert from the process go through the process. If you go through the process, God will make you Fall-proof. He will get you to the place where you are so dedicated to Him and the process that a fall is not in your future. Immaturity will make you walk in such arrogance that Proverbs 16:18 will be your reality. 1 Peter 5:5 says, "Young men are to submit to their Elders, showing reverence for their age and wisdom." Again, maturity will cause one to submit fully to someone who is seasoned in ministry. Submission is truly a key that you need and is necessary. One more thing concerning maturity, you can always determine one's maturity by the ones that are in their circle. If I stay linked to people that aren't going anywhere and don't carry the same convictions and values, it will cause me also to be stagnant.

Mentorship partnered with learning and development is essential for the Kingdom to be presented to the world. The reality is there has been a release of unlearned and untaught sons and daughters into the field of ministry. Again, it is most likely because of the ungodly motives that these unrighteous leaders have. One can be so focused on themselves that those that they show-boat as their sons and daughters don't receive any training from their leader. You would think if you wanted to put your son or daughter on display that you will teach them so that they would be established in the things of God. One true reality that I encountered was that the unrighteous that I was connected to could not impart because our DNA did not match. So where I was going in God, they had never been and could not contribute to my growth. Romans 1:11 "For I long to see you, that I may impart unto you some spiritual gift, to the end ye may be established;" I love this scripture because true righteous mentorship and partnership takes you to a place where you are established in your earthly ministry. Strong and pure impartation is imperative.

To my co-laborers in ministry, again remember not to lay hands on any person suddenly. Always be led by the Spirit of God of who you are setting and commissioning into ministry. Don't ignore the prompting and cautions of the Holy Spirit. Always check their reputation and character. What others say about them can be your RED flag? How they manage their household and personal affairs, should always be a determining factor in ordaining. And never ordain or release someone in ministry for your own personal gain.

To my emerging leaders in the Kingdom, remember to always walk in full integrity. Ministry is something that you must humble yourself and literally die to self, daily. Be conscious of your soul, and always operate in Godly motives. Practice what you preach; people can discern a hypocrite very easily. Ministry is not for you to make a name for yourself, but rather to glorify His name in all the earth. Don't be boastful or proud. Remember a title does not validate you, only the function and God's stamp of approval validates. Ministry calls for great mentorship and accountability. If you are too good to be mentored and held accountable, then ministry is not for you. You need to be covered. Seek God for who should spiritually cover you. If it is someone that wants to control, manipulate, and abuse you then they are not who God has ordained for your life.

Now let's raise up God's next General's and impact the Kingdom!

Prophetic Declaration: ***I decree and declare there are sons and daughters that are receiving true impartation for success in what the Father has called them to do. I declare that those that have attempted to skip the process of pruning and making will return to the process and complete it. I decree that God's people will not be released prematurely. Every person that has mishandled their spiritual sons and daughters are receiving another chance to pour into world-changers. The earth is still awaiting the manifestation of the sons of God and the sons are being birthed righteously.***

Chapter Five

Prophetic Preying

One of the most effective gifts used in the Body of Christ is that of prophecy. Prophecy is where one can obtain answers to unsolved questions and even direction. Prophecy according to 1 Corinthians 14:3 is God's way of bringing edification, encouragement, and comfort to the one on the receiving end. With every authentic expression from God, we must be on watch for the counterfeits that also come in the name of the Lord. Wolves are known to be false prophets who claim they are some great spokesperson for God. They claim they have been sent by God to release prophetic or divine inspiration from God. Their motive is not that the people that receive are edified, encouraged, or comforted but that their fleshly desires are fulfilled. Beware of the wolves. Matthew 7:15 says, "Beware of false prophets, who come to you in sheep's clothing, but inwardly are ravenous wolves." If we aren't careful, we will fall into their traps.

One thing that I notice is at work in our local assemblies is divination. Divination comes from the Latin word *divinare,* meaning "to foresee" or "to be inspired by a god. Wolves cannot see prophetically what is going on in a person's life, through the source of the Holy Spirit. So, they have to tap into a different realm. The source is a god but not the true and living God. This is why I call it prophetic preying. It is demonic and not of God. They are getting information from supernatural forces. It is associated with the occult. In ancient times, people would use divination to gain knowledge about the future or about people to obtain wealth. Any wolf operating in the church is only concerned with their personal gain.

So, could a wolf use divination to tap into one's struggle so that they can take advantage of them? Understand that the devil knows what you struggle with and will reveal it using familiar spirits. I call this not just prophetic preying but also demonic discernment partnered with divination. This brings me to the remembrance of a leader that I respected and looked up to as a mentor. He felt "led" to minister to me. He started with "Man of God, the Lord is calling you to the nations. You are a prophetic voice that God is going to give great influence." Please understand that the enemy is very cunning with his approach. The enemy opened me up to receive the "prophetic" word by first releasing words that I was used to hearing or saying words that I would want to hear because with all of the rejection I found validation in what I was called to do. It filled a void to know that I was important enough for God to use. So at this point, I was opened and in a vulnerable place. He proceeded to say he saw a great struggle in my life. A secret struggle that I was hiding but God was exposing it to him. He went on to say I see your attraction for men. I just sat there, and he asked does that make sense or is that true? Now, let's pause. I could have lied and said I don't know what you are talking about, or I could have said yes that's true because maybe God showed him this so that he could walk me through deliverance. So, shamefully I responded, "Yes sir, you are on point." He proceeded and said, Yes, I thought so." It didn't dawn on me at that time that he was asking me about my struggle because maybe, just maybe he dealt with the same thing. He went on to make me feel comfortable by saying, "Don't worry, I have been in the "life" too. I dealt with the same in my past." Of course to myself, I thought good, so he understands. He is so powerful and anointed, so I know he is going to help me out of this. Time progressed and days had passed since our initial conversation about my past. He always wanted to talk to me. Our times of connecting and talking on the phone became more frequently. He would often ask me details of my encounters. You know the who's, the what's, the when's, and most importantly the how's. Again, not fully thinking everything through I would openly share the details of everything that he would ask. It was not until years later that I had to ask what spirit revealed that to him. I honestly believe he was enjoying "getting off" by my pitfall. The conversations would shift to him now being transparent with me about his struggle. Of course, it was the same struggle. Before I go in any further, let me make something very clear. One cannot deliver another from the same spirit they are still dealing with. Demons don't cast out demons and perversion cannot confront perversion. This man of God and I say that loosely, used what he knew from whatever source he got it from to fulfill his nasty and perverted fantasies. And sadly, it worked and I fell. Can you imagine how many people in the church today are falling under this type of situation? Believe it or not, this is control and manipulation at its best. Many will say, "Harold, didn't you know?" My response would be, "No, I didn't." His approach was originally of one that was concerned and wanted to give me solutions on how to deal with the thorn in my flesh. So, he quickly gained my trust because I looked to him as a mentor, not a predator. He came masked as a concerned minister, but the true intent of his heart was to use what he knew about me through his demonic discernment. He was prophetically preying to have me sexually. How did his true motives come to light? One evening, we were on the phone chatting about my struggle and my past and to my surprise, he became bold and said that the things I was saying were turning him on. WHAT? This was the first time he had said this to me. And, from what I could tell he had "released" himself by masturbating. I could tell because he started moaning, and sounding very sexual in his tone.

Anyone in their right mind would have disconnected quickly, but I didn't because I was immersed in perversion. Knowing that someone of authority and power was interested in me, whether it was male or female, caused me to gain interest. Why? I was being accepted and didn't want to put myself in a position to be rejected. Things led to other things, meaning I fell into my predator's arms (literally). Even though I had moments of feeling accepted and loved, I would always still end up feeling empty.

Perversion will always leave you unsatisfied. The sinful satisfaction I found was only temporary.

Perversion creates patterns. I can remember using the same tactics that this predator used to get what I wanted. I would somehow pick up on the struggles of people that I was interested in. You know the discreet in the closet brothers and somehow would get them to come out to me. I would say stuff like the Lord showed me your issue. Just like how I fell into the arms of wolves, I became the wolves that did the same to me. I am so repentant, now.

When I joined Christian International Apostolic Network under the leadership of Dr. Bill Hamon, I loved the emphasis that they put on prophetic protocol. I especially appreciated the no "parking lot prophecies" policy. This is where people would prophesy to people outside of a place where seasoned senior leaders of the prophetic could first judge the word and the timing of it. Putting a stop to parking lot prophecies will protect the body of Christ from these predators that keep their "words from the Lord" from being heard by the seasoned leaders to prevent any type of prophetic preying. This has caused difficulty for those that have a true word from the Lord to release, because of the wounds that the body of Christ has obtained from false prophets. Many have become very hesitant to receive a "thus saith the Lord." If we would speak up when we notice this type of behavior in the church, it could stop the next person from falling prey to it.

There is another method that wolves use to get someone into their grip. They say the word is from their prophetic ability, but in all actuality it is gossip. Some leaders are going by what someone else exposed about the sheep to get them. They being just like the person that flows in divination go by what has been exposed and what they have heard by a 3rd party to start preying on the person they want. I personally know a pastor that had heard about my struggle through a mutual friend, and he attempted to invite me over to his house for some drinks and a good time. Apparently, he had speculated about my sexuality, so he went to my friend for confirmation. He got my friend to share it by masking it just like the other examples saying, "God told me this about Harold, what do you think?" My friend, unfortunately, opened up and told him it was true. And, I know what you are thinking, then was that a real friend? From there right before I almost fell into his arms or even his bed, I told my friend about the invite. He was surprised and luckily told me, "Well, Pastor asked me about you, and I told him. I asked, "Why did you tell him?" He said, "I really didn't tell him; I just confirmed it because he said God had already shown him. So, my friend felt obligated to release the information. See how all of this manipulation can cause some major confusion in a church body. Luckily, my friend spoke up, and I didn't fall into that trap. To see people free, we must raise our voices of justice. God is restoring integrity to the prophetic ministry.

Prophetic Declaration: ***I decree that the integrity of the prophetic is being restored. God is raising people to exhort, encourage, and comfort the people of God. I decree that the prophetic is being used for Kingdom gain, not personal gain. An integral prophetic company is being released. With this release, I declare and decree that the people of God would not be hesitant to receive. Everything false will be muted, and every true will be magnified. In this God will get the glory.***

Chapter Six

The Other Side of the Coin

Remember the story "The Boy Who Cried Wolf?" This young boy cried wolf several times and laughed when the people of the village came to help him. Then, he eventually needed them because the wolf was truly there and no one believed him, and the sheep were killed. When dealing with Spiritual abuse or unrighteous leadership, I have recognized that there is another side of the coin that we don't deal with, and that is the sheep that cries wolf. What I mean by this is not that they don't have a valid cry, but what they are calling abuse, misuse, or unrighteous may not necessarily be the case in the present, but could be an effect from the past. Most have been victims of turmoil by the hands of an abuser. The reality is that the abuser is often one that is close, whether it is a family member that physically or sexually abuses them or mental abuse by an authoritative figure like a pastor who uses their authority to benefit them. When a person does not confront the effects of their abuse, they will end up with a high spirit of offense.

They will feel everyone is out to abuse them and control them.

Have you ever come across someone who is always very negative when you try to connect or speak to them? Could it be that they have a hard time receiving you because you remind them of their past relationship or connection? They have become victims of past wolves, and they have not been able to free themselves from the wounds of the past.

When dealing with the sheep of God, we must be able to discern where they are in their process of healing and deliverance. If we are not careful, we will be accused of being a wolf in sheep's clothing or we will be deceived into thinking that someone else has been unrighteous to them. One term that is thrown out a lot is "church hurt" or "church abuse." When a leader righteously brings counsel, concern, or correction, one can believe in their heart that they are being manipulated. This could be that they have unresolved hurt from someone else before this leader, and they view all leaders the same as their abuser. So to them, everyone is out to get them. They have been offended and are holding unforgiveness in their heart.

Offense is defined as a violation, transgression, to hurt or to cause pain, to cause to fall into a sinful state. Many righteous leaders are being mistreated and disrespected because of the manipulation, control, and abuse of a previous leader. When a person has a strong spirit of offense on them, it is hard for them to see that they are hurting their God-ordained relationship. When you have gone through abuse of any sort, and haven't gone through deliverance, you will exemplify fear. And when you have this fear, you will do your best to put up a defense mechanism. This defense mechanism you feel will keep you from getting hurt or going through the same cycles. So, the ones that are showing you genuine love, you reject and believe they are just like the other ones. A practical example would be the wife that went through physical abuse, and now she is in a new relationship. Because of her past, she is very argumentative and downright nasty. The good guy now has to pay for the bad guy's mistakes. She views him as the guy that used to throw her body against the wall when that is not even his nature. Same thing goes for the sheep that are calling every leader they come in contact with a wolf, or everything that happens to them is an injustice. They were under a leader that was unethical and controlled them; now every leader must be the same.

Offense is a tool the enemy is using to throw the righteous, authentic, and loving leader in the same category as the unrighteous. If we are not careful and don't receive our wholeness in God, we will never be able to see the destiny-links and true blessings in our lives. We must recognize the spirit of offense and put it under the blood of Jesus so that we can see personal freedom. If you are a minister and have someone like this in your ministry, you mustn't reject them. You must maintain love, and offer them the deliverance they need. Yes, they maybe indignant and at times disrespectful, but they are crying out for help. Normally, you can notice if someone has been hurt and it's unresolved because they constantly talk about their past. One thing I have seen in the church is people tell hurt people to get over it and move on. We must show them how and give them the tools they need to help them. This is why deliverance is necessary. We must break people out of the bondage of their past relationships, their past abusive ministry coverings, and out of all the pain that is associated with it. Allowing offense and unresolved hurt to stay in the hurt will keep one stagnant, angry, and very fearful. When injustice is done, we have to let it go, resolve it immediately, forgive and move on (through deliverance). Otherwise, resentment, indignation, intolerance, and hatred will be present, and if we aren't careful, we will seek some form of revenge or restitution. But true breakthrough will cause a person to free and release freedom to others.

Discernment is always necessary when dealing with wounded sheep. Hebrews 5:14 "But solid food is for the mature, for those who have their powers of discernment trained by constant practice to distinguish good from evil." This is especially true when dealing with sheep that have been hindered by their past leaders because some walk in fear and will not release how they are truly feeling. In the past, I was so consumed by fear of authority. I always felt I had to be perfect. Even as a man, I felt like I had to ask permission for every move I made to protect myself from rejection or anything that could position me for abandonment. I was so consumed that when people gave me counsel, I felt consumed with pressure to do exactly what they said, when they said, and how they said it should be done. I say this because sometimes we can be so consumed that we are afraid to speak up for help. I believe God is releasing an army of leaders that have the discernment to pick up the past of someone else, not for shame but assisting them with their breakthrough. I am reminded of when I first started going through deliverance from my past of being under unrighteous leaders. I attended the International Training Center in Elizabethville, PA. It was a training school preparing leaders for the future. This was my place of safety, after going through so much with wolves. One evening the school was hosting an apostle of the Lord, Apostle Louis Dickens. God used Apostle Louis in a unique way, especially because of my past with men in ministry. I was not always receptive to a male ministering to me. God gave Apostle Louis specific prophetic words that I knew was only from God. He kept speaking of the wolves from my past, specifically in the religious arenas. As he hit certain areas of my life, I began to manifest. Demons began to scream out, demons of hurt, rejection, perversion, religiosity, and fear. And at that point, Apostle Louis began administering deliverance. When it was all said and done, I felt like 500 pounds were lifted off me, and I knew that it was a feeling of true freedom. No more bondage, chains, or fear!

I will be the first to admit the obvious, wolf bites hurt. If discernment is not used and pure leadership doesn't show up, the victim is in huge trouble. From everything that I dealt with, I was very depressed and hurt. When I had to deal with someone of spiritual authority, I always had a fear that they would turn on me. Fear plagued me so much that I became suicidal. I attempted suicide on several occasions because I could no longer take the pain of being used like I was just a possession of someone. I had such a false perception of spiritual leaders. I put them all in a category of wolves. Casual conversations about leaders would turn into me bashing the leaders, no matter who they were. I know how the young lady feels that believes in her heart that all men are dogs, because of the hurt that she experienced. I went through a season that in my eyes, all leaders were wolves. You may say that is very judgmental, or a bad perception to have, but it was where I was. My vulnerability had me going from covering to covering getting bit and bit some more. So the other side of the coin is, that I began to cry wolf even when I wasn't in the presence of the wolves. I felt that I was not valuable enough to experience Godly love with no bad motives from spiritual leaders. Every experience wounded me; we are talking about a cycle of being under about four different coverings with bad experiences.

There is serious soul issues tied to spiritual abuse. If I had never confronted my soul issue of hate towards leadership, I would never be able to be a real godly leader to his people. I would most likely repeat the behaviors that were modeled. I so appreciate the deliverance I experienced from the hurt. Apostle Louis took me through the healing and deliverance process, but if I had never made up in my mind to forgive and to be healed, I would be a messed up person today. One thing that gives me joy today is for my abusers to see that I am whole and I have forgiven them. It still makes me laugh when I cross paths with one of them, and they don't see the broken Harold, but they see the Harold that God has made me to be. And you can tell they are standing there surprised. There was a time where I probably wanted to kill them or set up some type of humiliation for them, but God came and changed my heart.

Can you do me a favor? If you have been a victim and you still have that hurt and hate in you, find your deliverance before it is too late. It is not your job to try to get revenge, but it is your job to get free through Him. Or if you are someone that has someone in your life that you hear the cry of wolf, show them the love of Christ and believe with them for healing.

The church could be a better place if we let the river of healing and deliverance flow. Wolves are being exposed, and the people of God are being healed.

Prophetic Declaration: ***I decree and declare that those that have experienced injustice are receiving the healing from the Master that they need. The victim mentally is being cut off, and the people are living free from the offense of their trespassers of the past. Any negative perception of the church, from pain the people have endured, is being reconfigured because the church is the bride of Christ. I affirm that the church of God is being restored to God's original design. With this, God's hurting people are being restored to their original design mapped out by God.***

Chapter Seven

The Return

As I mentioned in the previous chapter, I attended the International Training Center as a resident student. I was so excited for a fresh start. I initially struggled to adjust to their CORE values. They were definitely Spirit-led leaders. I was so used to religiosity that their ways at times irked my nerves. You know why because they were big on accountability and Godly discipline. I see, today, that they were looking to develop quality leaders, it went way beyond titles or positions it was about integrity and character. I went to the school already ordained, so certain things they taught I felt I was above it and often bucked against and challenged my leaders there at the school. They were always patient and loving towards me, but I was a little hellion.

One day, I woke up with extreme pain in my side. I immediately called my mother and stepfather. They wanted me to come home and see a doctor. So, one of my cousins drove the 2.5 hours to pick me up. I returned home. When I returned home, I went to the doctors and they discovered I had kidney stones. So, I went through a procedure and had to take a few weeks away from the school. When I returned home, people from my old church, you remember the wolves I had danced with for years found out I was home. When I was at the school, I remember hearing God tell me to never reconnect with these wolves again. Remember that deliverance session I had with Apostle Louis? I was set, my mind was made up, and I was never going to return to being a victim of all of the control, manipulation, perversion, and abuse again. I have learned that you can make up something in your mind, but the residue of your past could activate desires to go back. So after not much time, I returned to the church or the den of wolves and never returned to the school. I gave up the safety to go back with danger. What in the world was in me? Why did I want to become prey again? What is in a person that has been abused whether sexually, verbally, mentally, or even spiritually to return to the same cycle? This is one of the greatest weapons the enemy uses, and that is to cause people to go back to what God has taken them from.

So, why did I return? The first thing I dealt with was denial. I started saying to myself they didn't do anything bad to me these people love me, and I need to go ahead back home. I was in 100% denial of everything that I had dealt with and even sometimes blamed myself for it. I was in denial, and even my leadership and associates were in denial of the spiritual abuse. The reality is that this was a cult. I lacked the ability to see the truth and what I was going through. As for me, it was familiarity. I returned back to what I knew. Remember when I was at the International Training Center, they were doing things I wasn't familiar with so going back home was so comfortable. I remember I couldn't wait to get back to my old church to get a good dance in, and I sure did. I danced and danced until I couldn't dance anymore thinking this was where I belonged, forgetting that this was the place that most of my heartaches came from. So not only familiarity, but this was the place that I felt accepted and celebrated because of my ability to preach, prophesy, and teach. So, why not return?

My desire to go back to the perversion, control and manipulation was not just a spiritual battle it was also physiological. As I studied on why abused victims return, I came across a physiological term I had never heard before, Stockholm syndrome. Stockholm syndrome is defined in the Merriam-Webster dictionary as, "the psychological tendency of a hostage to bond with, identify with, or sympathize with his or her captor. This syndrome ties people together intimately and emotionally despite the danger that it puts the victim in. I was sick, and never even knew it. I just thought I was supposed to be connected to the bishop, my ex, and the church. Even though these were the reasons, I experienced so much hurt and pain. So, I ignored the past. I had a distorted understanding of forgiveness by forgiving them and letting my guards down and getting right back in the posture to be attacked by the wolves again. When I studied even deeper the Stockholm Syndrome, The medical dictionary advises that this syndrome comes from a bank robbery in Stockholm Sweden, in August 1973. The robber took four employees of the bank into the vault and kept them hostage for 131 hours. After they had been released, those that were captive formed an emotional bond with the captor. They said they saw the police as their enemy, not the bank robber, and that they had positive feelings toward the criminal. This brings me to an excellent point. I remember when I left the school and knew I wasn't returning. The school had recommended that I connect to a powerful ministry couple, Apostles Michael and Donna Scott of Bethel Worship Center in Frederick, MD, my hometown. They were real, and they were attempting to rescue me from the cycle that I just returned to. They would call me, check on me, even bring me to Bible studies and worship services. But, I viewed them as trying to take me from where I felt I was supposed to be. One thing that I celebrate today is that even though I shut this couple out of my life, they maintained a love for me, care for me, and are in my life today.

When I initially left my home church, there were seeds of guilt, and words of curses spoken over me. Of course, this is a method that a lot of religious leaders use to cause you to be afraid to leave them. I left, but I could always hear them say, "Your ministry is going to fail, you are rebellious for leaving us, God is not going to bless you, you are cursed, and you belong with us." Words have so much power. I believe that when I was debating to return to the church, I didn't want to fail, or be viewed as rebellious, and wanted to live under an open heaven of blessings, so I returned to what once destroyed me to almost death. Their word curses assisted in me making my decision to return, and it worked. I even remember one minister coming to me saying you are the Apple of Bishop's eye and you hurt him by leaving. You need to return to your father. He needs you, and you need him.

I also remember how all of the ones that cut me off and didn't want to speak to me started calling and texting wanting to reconnect. Could this be a strategy my leader used or the enemy used? Yes, most likely. They started making me feel a part again. I was like wow, I have friends again. It was devastating what I felt when I left the church, and the people stopped speaking to me. Not to mention my full ministry schedule dropped to the point where I would be lucky if I received an invite to preach once every three months. It weighed on me. Because so many people were so loyal to the Bishop, they attempted to shut doors on me. Now, with the thought of me returning my preaching schedule grew again, people were accepting me again. It felt like God. Maybe I am supposed to be back, is what I said to myself. Everything looks like it is falling back in place, and I am starting to be the hottest commodity.

One evening, the Bishop called me. He said, "Son, I feel like you are supposed to minister this Sunday." I thought oh wow. Yes, sir, I will minister. And, we ended the call. I was so pumped. This return was not in vain. Even the Bishop believes I am supposed to be back and has asked me to preach this weekend. Let me call everyone and invite them. Let me preach my face-off. I want these people to see what I have in me. These were all the thoughts that went through my head. So, I prepared to preach. I had a word I felt was straight from the Lord. If I can remember correctly, it was most likely an emotional sermon that I knew would end with the saints dancing and shouting all over the church. I was ready.

That Sunday, I woke up ready to minister. I brought out my best looking suit and shiny shoes. Worship was awesome as always. As I looked from the pulpit, I was amazed. The place was packed. Before I knew it, the Bishop was introducing me to come up and preach. I had no nervousness in me. I was ready to work this text and bless the people. I grabbed the mic and placed my Bible and notes on the podium, but something strange started happening to me. I started shaking, and I couldn't even greet the congregation. As I attempted to speak, all I could do was cry hysterically. Okay, first of all, this was embarrassing, and I had to get this word out, I was saying to myself. The more I tried to speak the more I would weep until I was buckled over and the Bishop came and embraced me. The church went into worship. I don't think they knew what was going on. I never even got to preach. What just happened? The bishop said I was supposed to preach so what happened?

A few days later, I felt the Holy Spirit wanted to share something with me in private. I felt that He was saying that I was trying to fit myself back into a place where he had delivered me from. I heard something even more clearly, "You mustn't attempt to put yourself in a mold and a system that you do not fit, and YOU DO NOT BELONG." Of course, I knew He was referring to returning to the church. I had to leave the church, never to be a part of the membership again. So, I left the church. This time the bishop called me back and wanted to release me. I lied to them and told them the only reason I was leaving was because I felt a call to pastor. The real reason was because God told me to leave this time and never to return. So, they released me, laid hands on me and told the church I was starting my own church. I did start my church and it went well, the only thing was I begin to model the broken system I was accustomed to. I pastored for six years until the Lord called me away from pastoring to join my spiritual parent's church of which I am a part of today. Of course, I still minister, but I have a place I call home with no negative strings attached. They support the apostolic ministry on my life.

My return to the place I thought was home could have ended very drastically. I think if I would have sat there any longer that I would have lost my mind, hurt myself or someone else. One thing that I appreciate is that when I go back several years to the International Training Center days, there were Godly seeds planted, which caused me to return to Apostle Steven and Dr. Melodye who pioneered that school and spoke prophetic words over a broken, hurt, wounded young man. Now, I am their spiritual son, healed, delivered, and set free impacting the marketplace and churches. They could have given up on me, when I left the school and returned to the place where the wolves danced. But, when I came back around almost ten years later, they welcomed me to be a part of the Apostolic Network and the church with open arms. Since returning, I have received the righteous impartation needed, necessary rebukes, and

Godly love. I never thought that I would be accepted by real, honest leaders. The shame and guilt of my past tried to keep me from reaching out to Apostle Melodye. I am so glad that when I did, she was so loving and accepting. Then my wife and I had lunch with both she and Apostle Steven. At that point, I knew that God took me full circle back to place where I truly belonged.

After reconnecting with Apostle Steven and Dr. Melodye the Lord began to do a serious reprogramming in me. He started to deal with me first as a person. I will be the first to admit that I didn't like being dealt with by the Holy Spirit. He changed my whole understanding of family and ministry. It was so strange because I knew the Lord was calling me away from pastoring my local assembly. It was tough to swallow. He kept saying I want to do a new thing in you. So, I listened to the leading of the Holy Spirit. I started speaking to my wife about it, she was in agreement. Then I went to my leaders, and they also agreed and supported what I felt God was saying. Then the hard part, I went to my church family and told them that I would be shifting out of pastoring. It was hard, but most of them understood what God was doing. He was working on me and preparing me for a greater place in Him. So, I resigned as the senior pastor. This gave me time to see the true essence of family and ministry. This was a time where all of the unrighteous impartation that I had received would be blotted out me. I must also admit that I had that religious spirit, but God worked on me. One thing I noticed during this time was there was a greater sense of healing, and even my family was being made whole from the effects of pastoring a ministry. Let me make one thing clear, no, I have not arrived, but I am no longer that broken, hateful, prideful leader that I was years ago. I am open now to the leading of the Holy Spirit like never before. When you ask God to make you over, then you move yourself out of the way. It makes things progress so much faster in your life.

Prophetic Declaration: ***I decree and declare that any false responsibilities placed on any victim to return to their place of pain would be taken off in Jesus name. I decree that God has risen up places of worship that individuals can connect to that would not repeat the cycle of hurt that they have experienced. I declare that just because one ministry has done them wrong, does not mean that all are the same. God is restoring His church through His glory.***

Chapter Eight

Accounts

Throughout the book, I have given my story and my testimony. I still believe Revelation 12:11. It says, "And they overcame him by the blood of the Lamb, and by the word of their testimony, and they loved not their lives unto death. I have had the opportunity to interview several individuals and with their consent, I have chosen to include these accounts with you. They all were asked the same series of questions. Often when dealing with spiritual abuse and the act of dancing with wolves, you feel like you are all alone, and this only happened to you. The victims and their abusers will remain confidential..

Let these real life experiences/accounts be an eye opener for each and every reader. You may even find yourself being able to relate.

Account #1

1. **Can you describe to me the type of spiritual abuse you encountered?**

"The spiritual abuse I encountered was more so manipulation and control."

2. **Who was the abuser (their position not name)?**
"My former Apostle submitted to under his leadership and covering."

3. **What specifically happened? How were you abused?**
"The Apostle lacked the ability or desire to pour into me, and when it came to me sharing what I was called to do, I was told that ministry is not for everyone. He totally disregarded what I felt the Lord was saying to me. He advised that God would need to show it to him first as my leader for it to be deemed authentic before showing it to me. It also affected my marriage. He would share stuff with my wife about me to bring confusion. He did one of the most damaging things to me. He advised my wife that I had chosen ministry over her. He was attempting to shut down my voice. He also went to other pastors and shared things with them about me that I shared with him in confidence. He also made up lies to cause people to disconnect with me. The Apostle's friends now treated me differently. They showed me a different attitude, which demonstrated

that he said some negative things about me. He reprimanded me in front of my CORE leadership team and told me that I needed to shut down my church and manipulated scripture to back up his control. He went on to say that if I didn't shut down my church and sit under him at his church for a year or so then he would no longer cover me."

4. **How did you feel about the abuse?**

   "At first, I didn't want to live anymore. I also felt like I didn't want to serve God anymore. I couldn't understand why God would allow this to happen to me again because I dealt with this before from other leaders and trusted this leader that he would not repeat my past experiences. I felt like giving up on everything my life, marriage and my ministry."

5. **What do you think contributed to you falling into the trap?**

   "I believe that I, unfortunately, had a lack of discernment. This affected my ability in choosing the proper leadership for my family and me. Also my desire for covering without taking the proper steps to ensure they were the right leader. I also feel that maybe God had me under that type of leadership to learn what not do."

6. **How did you escape?**

   "When I shared with a prophet friend of mine what happened with my Apostle, he decided to do a periscope broadcast around controlling leadership. From there someone under the covering of my apostle reached out to him and advised of the periscope that she had just viewed and she felt it was towards Apostle. This lady operated in a Jezebelic spirit and always brought some type of confusion. When the apostle learned of the periscope broadcast, he felt it was directed to him. He then called me and released me from his covering and questioned my integrity."

7. **How did you recover?**

   "It took months to recover, through prayer and people encouraging and pouring into me. They advised me to never give up and not to let go of the vision that God put inside of me. I held on to the promises of God."

8. **If you could say anything to your abuser today, what would it be?**

   "I forgive you, and I release the situation over to God. Just because I forgive doesn't mean reconciliation. Unfortunately, I will never trust him again."

9. **If you could give words of wisdom to someone being abused what would you say?**

   "Before you make the decision to join a fellowship or ministry, do some serious praying make sure God is telling you to connect. This is not to discourage you from submitting to a leader but to help you avoid going through what I went through."

Account #2

1. **Can you describe to me the type of spiritual abuse you encountered?**

"I lived with pastors that were like spiritual parents to me and the husband took advantage of me physically and mentally."

2. **Who was the abuser (their position not name)?**

"The pastor was a worship leader and I was a part of the worship team."

3. **Who was the abuser (their position not name)?**

"One night while home alone, the pastor and I were sitting on the couch and he rubbed my leg inappropriately and then pulled back my shirt to expose my breast. From there, he'd just continue to approach me whenever we were home alone and the sexual interaction would get more intense. The manipulation and mental abuse came from my opening up to him about the poor relationship that I had with my father and how I looked up to him and appreciated the relationship that we had. I felt like he used that to prey on me. He would always talk about how he wished that he was younger because he would've dated or married me. He also would always talk about his wife's weight issues and compliment me on my body."

4. **How did you feel about the abuse?**

"The abuse made me feel rejected, worthless. Every girl wants to be loved by her father. It wasn't that my real father didn't love me but his drug addiction and suicidal attempts really put a strain on our relationship. To have finally had someone in my life that I looked up to as a father turn on me like that made me feel unloved. Also, this pastor was MUCH older than me so it made me feel unattractive like I was undesirable to men my own age."

5. **What do you think contributed to you falling into the trap?**

"Trust! I knew this pastor for several years. His daughter was my best friend. I lived with them. They were just like parents to me. When this happened, I was very confused and couldn't understand why he'd do such a thing."

6. **How did you escape?**

"I was very depressed as I endured a few months in this situation. I wanted to die. I finally got enough courage to tell his daughter and then I moved out of their house."

7. **How did you recover?**

"I know many people have anger and hatred towards their abuser, but I for some reason never felt that. I immediately forgave this pastor and spent those following months after exposing him and leaving his home praying for him. I found out that he was fired from his current pastoral position, that his family and marriage was in an uproar, and that he admitted to having many other sexual encounters with women. I wanted to be mad but I knew deep down that this man was an anointed man of God with a call on his life with a flaw just like the rest of us. I wanted God to heal and deliver him and turn what Satan meant for evil into something good. I thank God that my heart was not hardened to God or church. God gave me a heart of love that allowed me to forgive because forgiveness and interceding for this pastor and his family made way for Daddy God to heal my heart."

8. If you could say anything to your abuser today, what would it be?

"I forgive you and if you haven't already done so, forgive yourself."

9. If you could give words of wisdom to someone being abused what would you say?

"Quickly forgive. Forgiveness doesn't discount your feelings or what you've been through, but it does free you from the plan of the enemy to keep you in bondage. While you may want revenge or ill wishes on your abuser remember that the Word says in Matthew 6:14-15. "For if you forgive other people when they sin against you, your heavenly Father will also forgive you. But if you do not forgive others their sins, your Father will not forgive your sins."

"Also, I know everyone may not agree with me but I always believe that most people don't just wake up and think I am going to abuse, molest, kill, or harm someone today. Most people who do these things have had something happen to them that they haven't dealt with or been healed from, and they are doing these things as a result of those undealt with issues. This is especially true in the case of sexual abuse. Having this perspective was also a huge contributor to me recovering from what happened to me."

Account #3

1. **Can you describe to me the type of spiritual abuse you encountered?**
   "While being a member of a church, God would reveal things to me about the church. God called me to work with the leaders and expose what was in the leadership. When I would tell them what God was saying, the leaders' spouse would get upset and clearly show that she didn't care for me. She would even go on rants and tell me that I thought I was cute. She would verbally abuse me."

2. **Who was the abuser (their position not name)?**
   "The Pastor's wife"

3. **What specifically happened? How were you abused?**
   "The pastor's wife was always attacking me verbally to make me feel like I was nobody. To bring more problems to me she would pretend like she would want to minister to me, but because of her hate towards me, she would tell me things contrary to the word of God, even to the point of interfering and bringing division within my marriage and family life. She would always give me "advice" that would have a bad result. She would always do the opposite of what she would tell me to do. Every single function they would come to me, and "minister" to me but at the same time they would be talking about me in their cliques and leading me different directions. I wondered why I was there, the old me wanted to cuss them out and fight, but the new me was being humbled. I even remember one day I volunteered to clean the church and just to give me a hard time and to make me do it over and over again she would say I wasn't cleaning it well. So they were very aggressive to

me. I would be in the middle of cleaning and I would look up and they would be standing there talking about me, laughing and snickering. She was threatened that I would take her husband from her, so she became a bully in the church."

4. **How did you feel about the abuse?**
   "I was very hurt and disgusted. This is the worst I have ever felt being in church rather than out. I felt most inadequate in church than out."
5. **What do you think contributed to you falling into the trap?**
   "I had a strong desire to be obedient to God but failed to keep my guard up. I believe it was more so her insecurities about my looks and her fear of something happening between her husband and me."
6. **How did you escape?**
   "True men of God were used by God and exposed what was going on. God used the prophetic to reaffirm who I was in the Lord."
7. **How did you recover?**
   "God begin to reveal stuff to me prophetically that confirmed what the men of God said. I know that the adversary tried to use what was done to me to

stop me, but God used this to get me to go where He was calling me. I also had a family member that I was able to confide in. He was able to minister to my spirit in the way that brought my desired healing."

8. **If you could say anything to your abuser today, what would it be?**

"I would tell the couple that it is vitally important that they love every person with agape love. If you have any issues with anyone personally, you need to go to them in love. If you are treating people maliciously because of what they look like or what they wear, then it will be noticed and you could be keeping others from wanting to be a part of your ministry. You are blocking what they are supposed to receive from your church and you are going to be held accountable for holding back what they are supposed to be receiving. This is a test for you. To my former pastor or any pastor, your spouse can hurt your church and your destiny if you let them. Seek God when your spouse is manipulating you and your church. Discipline your spouse as you teach us to discipline."

9. **If you could give words of wisdom to someone being abused what would you say?**
   "God always speak to us, sit somewhere quiet and listen to what He says. Sometimes, He will call you to the cave to yourself. He will tell you where to go and who to connect with. And, that is how you flourish and can be on your way and active in your God-given mission. God told me that your trials are your tests, your tests are your testimony and your testimony is your ministry. Everyone has a ministry in them even if it is a ministry of reconciliation. Seek God first, that way the devil can't kill your dream, steal your joy and destroy your destiny."

Account #4

1. **Can you describe to me the type of spiritual abuse you encountered?**
   "Most of the abuse I have encountered was mental and eventually led to sexual. There was a lot of manipulation and control involved."
2. **Who was the abuser (their position not name)?**
   "My abuser was an Apostle I sat under for almost three years."

3. **What specifically happened? How were you abused**

"The Apostle and I met in an unusual way. I met the Apostle on a gay/bisexual website about two years prior to me coming to his ministry. His name on the website was "Jay." We became very close friends and he picked me up almost every other day to hang out, there was nothing sexual. I felt comfortable enough to share my personal issues with him and the things that were going on with my family and the church I was attending. At this particular time, he didn't mention to me that he was a pastor nor did he mention that he was an apostle. As a matter of fact, because of where I came from I didn't know there was even such a thing as a modern day Apostle. To make a long story short, I found out that he was married and an apostle. This was after we became so close that I could not separate. Something dramatic happened in my old ministry, so my plan was to go back into the world because of the damage that was done to me. At one point we separated because the marriage thing bothered me. I didn't feel like that was ok. Somehow, we ended up getting back in contact with each other. He invited me to his ministry. This is when I found out who he really was. Now that he was my pastor, I didn't want any sexual contact, so I stayed away from any personal contact. His ministry was very family-oriented. I met his mother who is a fire and brimstone apostle. He kept inviting me to his home which I refused. Finally, his mother invited me, which I thought was weird considering she knew of her son's struggle. He assured me that nothing would happen, so I took the bait. We ended up in his basement and this is where the sexual encounter happened. I felt bad, and he promised it would never happen again. One thing I noticed was that he and his wife didn't sleep in same room. He told me they were getting a divorce which was a lie. Trouble also began to arise in his ministry. Much jealousy and envy from those in his family. Any issues that arose between him and his family he sided with them and not me. The people wanted to fight me in the church as well as in the home. At this point, I wanted to go home because of all of this, but he would not allow me to leave. He didn't want me to connect with other church leaders or even my own family. He claimed that every time I came from my family's home that I would bring a spirit back with me. I had to be with him 24/7. I even quit my job trying to be a support to him because he wanted to hire me full time. But, that turned out to be a control device because I had to eat when he wanted me to eat and sleep when he wanted me to sleep. I couldn't go anywhere without someone being with me even if I was going to see my family. I began to have issues within myself because I was looking for an outlet. I felt like if I would leave or leave wrong something would happen to me. One thing I noticed was that when people left him, they would die."

4. **How did you feel about the abuse?**

   "In my mind, I wrestled with the thought of how to get away. Every attempt to go somewhere was pointless because someone had to follow me or he had to be present. Even the sexual encounters were more intense. He made me feel like he was using me as a sex slave. He tried to cover up our relationship by making me his armor bearer. There was one point in the ministry where I just wanted to run for my life. That's when I noticed I was in mental bondage."

5. **What do you think contributed to you falling into the trap?**

   "I think my issue was I didn't know any other pastors, so I stayed and just had to deal with the problems facing me. I also didn't want to be viewed as a "church hopper." When I took the bait by going to his house is when I fell into the trap. I believe if I didn't take the bait, things with him might have turned out a little different but I'm sure he would've found another method to get within proximity of me."

6. **How did you escape?**

   "A prophetess/Seer joined our ministry and exposed everything that was going on in the dark. Around this time mentally I was done, I just wanted out and prayed for a way of escape. After the exposure, the sexual encounters stopped. The Apostle started to pick at me openly; he was mad one day because I went to see a few of my friends. At this point, I was through and I decided to get up and walk out the door never to return. He would call and text me non-stop. When he noticed I wasn't coming back, he told everyone to delete me off of Facebook. He damaged my name and I was damaged goods beyond repair. One day, I laid in my bed and heard different people praying. I knew who they were and they were actually praying death over me. After their prayers, I was hospitalized. He sent two members from the church to the hospital, but he stayed in his car. A couple of days later my little brother was killed. When he found this out, he asked to see me. He wanted to meet at a hotel. I said no."

7. **How did you recover?**

   "After my brother's death, I moved out of state to recover. I began to pray and build myself back up. I had to change my scenery to recover. I cried to God daily asking Him, "Why me?"

8. **If you could say anything to your abuser today, what would it be?**

   "I have reached out to him to let him know I forgive him and that I am moving forward."

9. **If you could give words of wisdom to someone being abused what would you say?**

   "Ask God for a way of escape and run like your life depends on it. Don't avoid the warning signs. Get out while you still have time."

Prophetic Declaration: ***I decree and declare as people are confronting their past and those that have wronged them, that they do not receive any retaliation from the enemy or their abusers. People are speaking forth truth to bring about healing and to ensure the same behavior doesn't happen to anyone else. We decree a continued boldness and no compromise within the body of Christ. God is healing his people and releasing them from the chains of darkness.***

Chapter Nine

Righteous Impartation

A doctrine was formulated to judge one's legitimacy in the ministry called "Apostolic Succession." The practice of "Apostolic Succession" is one that was derived from the Catholic Church and now has been accepted and practiced in a lot of the African American ministry fellowships, and or organizations. Apostolic succession is the belief that the 12 apostles passed down their authority to their successors who then repeated this throughout centuries and generation. In Apostolic Succession, the Apostle Peter is viewed as the apostle leader of all apostles with the greatest authority. This is very popular with Bishop Consecration services. That from one Bishop consecrating another that they can trace their consecration lineage back to Peter. During these consecrations, they lay hands and pass the authority to the newly consecrated Bishop. Because of this becoming such a popular belief, Prominent African American Bishops went to England to get linked into this line of succession. This is a man-made and a money scheme initiative. As much as I honor and respect the original apostles, I believe this is just another way to fatten the pockets of the modern day religious, unrighteous leaders today. This is another example of manipulation in the church. If you do not link up with the doctrine and go through the steps, you are considered illegitimate. Let me make one thing clear before we move into this chapter that legitimacy and promotion comes from the Lord first, and is confirmed by other Righteous leaders.

Legitimacy to me has nothing to do with if a person can trace their ministry back to the Apostle Peter. The true mark of legitimacy and success is one's character traced back to Christ. Now, that is a notion that should proceed to succession. As I believe in receiving an impartation from your spiritual leader, if the focus is only to trace our lineage back to Peter, we are missing something key. We need to ensure we can trace our actions back to Christ and that the actions of our leaders show Christ.

Could it be possible that there are un-repented sins from your spiritual fathers or mothers that have been overlooked, or masked with religion that is now being passed down to you? Spiritual parenting and covering is essential for the success of one's ministry. But often times, young preachers are pressured to get a covering and they end up connecting with the wrong "spiritual parent." The young minister tends to flock to the most popular well-known leader and the connection may be more of a destiny blocker than a destiny link. A major function of a spiritual parent is to pass their mantle. If not careful a mantle can have a sinful nature intertwined within it. You must check who your spiritual leader is both in the natural and in the spiritual. What does their reputation say about them?

When a person is interested in connecting with a specific network, the senior leaders do a background check on a person's integrity and character. I believe this is a good practice, and I suggest that when joining an organization or considering a specific covering that proper research is completed before making the decision. In this day, you have to check their background, their spiritual lineage, are they still in the sin, etc. If you don't check someone, you could wake up one day dealing with the same tendencies and issues that your spiritual father's father had. Check the oil that's running down on your life and ministry. You do not have the choice of who your natural parents are but you do have a say of who your spiritual parents are. The key is to always be led by the Holy Spirit.

I remember when I started attending that church where I became very much involved and became a minister on staff. I truly wish I would have done some research on the Senior Pastor, the former pastor and the church history. As time progressed, I began to notice that many of the members more specifically the males dealt with some sexual perversion. This was a Holiness Pentecostal church, where sin was preached against so tell me how so many people could be struggling in perversion, but deliverance was nowhere to be found? Could it be that the preaching of it was just to cover up the true condition of the church and the leadership? When sin has infiltrated the very foundation and culture of a ministry, two things can happen from the pulpit. The first is that the Senior Leadership will preach seeker friendly sermons that never address the SIN. With this, they want to play it safe because they don't want to expose their own sin by preaching against it. Have you ever sat in a church that all they preach about is blessings but they never hit on the fact that blessings may be held up because of the sin that is in the camp? The second thing that I have done is preached so hard on the subject of perversion to give the illusion that I, myself wasn't in the sin. For example, I would preach about homosexuality so much and I would become so raw with it that I would call people in the lifestyle homos, faggots, or even punks. Again, if I preached on it like that I was presenting the message like I hated the sin but the reality was I would leave a service after preaching like that and partake in the things that I preached against. And I was not held accountable for my actions, again because my gift masked my perversion. The need for righteous impartation is essential for any leader.

Righteous impartation is so important that we see a great example of this with Elijah and Elisha in 2 Kings. Elisha wanted what was in Elijah and was willing to sacrifice for Godly impartation. God had already called him a prophet but Elisha understood that impartation would bring a greater awareness and maximization to the effectiveness of his ministry. I believe Elisha had pure motives and recognized that Elijah was his destiny link. Elisha was led by the Spirit of God to connect to Elijah and not waver to the left or right. He was also drawn to Elijah because he saw the reputation and heart of his leader. We must look at who we are submitted to as our spiritual authority/covering and began to evaluate if their impartation is bringing effectiveness or ineffectiveness, stagnation or major growth and progression. A righteous spiritual father/mother doesn't look for what they can get from you, but rather what they can impart to you that will release you into a greater place. The greatest gift to me as a spiritual father is to see my sons and daughters flowing freely in their kingdom purpose.

Now we can't put all the responsibility of the impartation and the passing down of the mantle to the spiritual parent. As a son/daughter there is responsibility on your part as well. Elisha stayed in constant fellowship and showed his loyalty. Many are loyal to dysfunctional relationships but neglect true righteous leadership. So again, like Elisha, you must discern why you are connected to your leader. Is it just a connection or is it a covenant? Connections based on the motives and hearts of the individuals can be based on convenience. Don't waste your time by being loyal to someone that is a priority to you, but you are not a priority to them. They must be an asset to your life and not a liability. Covenant relationships are righteous driven. Covenant is based on a greater good and purpose and lasts into eternity. Elisha was willing to go with Elijah until death; unfortunately, we don't see this much today. Often when a leader corrects their follower, which is a part of righteous impartation, the follower forfeits the relationship and moves to the next leader that will stroke their ego and "cover" their mistakes rather than teach them. This book is about unrighteous leadership, but unrighteous followers are also evident in Christendom today. Elijah tried to get Elisha to stay back on a lot of the ministry trips; I believe he was testing the authenticity of the relationship and if Elisha truly valued the impartation of Elijah. Other prophets tried to sway him away but Elisha was not moved by the opinions of others. This reminds me of a situation that I was in. A good friend of mine, who was looking out for me, recommended that I submitted under a specific leader for covering. Can I be honest? It was the worst move I had ever made. I submitted to this wolf, and I didn't know anything about him. After a little while, the true motives of his heart came out, and he was very controlling. I quickly disconnected. I just want to encourage you to stay committed and obedient to the voice of God and he will lead you to your Elijah! Elisha was committed to the process and whatever it would bring. With struggles, battles, testing, and triumphs commitment is key! I can almost guarantee that if your covering is more concerned about a financial obligation but lacks relational connections, then they are a wolf. The truth is wolves eventually will kill you.

Sin in the church becomes a learned inherited behavior. Why? That is simply because of perversion and lack of accountability. Many unrighteous leaders themselves are full of deception and aren't accountable. They are competing for the next big position or title. If you have to compete for a position, then you are affecting your ability to flow in the true assignment that God has called you too. I believe a lot of people don't want impartation; they just want opportunity and promotion. I have seen ministers receive a promotion from man through acts of perversion. They have preached their way up, crept their way up, and even slept their way up. Compromise is a tool for the title-hungry to get what they want. We must be so committed to Christ and the call on our lives to receive the succession and baton in the right spirit. If succession is not given by the good, then succession is not succession it is DAMNATION!

Do you know what scares me so much? Is when a son/daughter knows about the current sin their leader is in but they turn their eyes away for the cost of promotion? This is dangerous. No promotion or succession is worth being in connection to dangerous wolves. You are dancing with Wolves just like I did for many years. It took a long time for me to trust again. Not to mention, shame was associated with it all. I recognized that the cycle had to be broken off of my life, I had to open up to receive from righteous leadership, and then turn around and model that which I needed. I knew as the song "Song of Intercession" by William McDowell says, "The change I want to see must first begin in me, I surrender so your world can be changed." Righteousness had to be released in me and through me. My healing came because of my motivation to see others healed.

Prophetic Declaration: ***I decree and declare righteous Elijah's are arising with pure impartation to release. Righteous Elisha's are also arising to receive the pure impartation that is being released. Destiny links are being uncovered and the recipients are pursuing these links with all sincerity and no hidden motives. This Elijah's whether male or female are ready to do the kingdom work, and will not only receive righteously but will also give out righteously to the next generation of revival starters and reformers.***

Chapter Ten

Righteous Leader Arise

When you have seen nothing but perverted, manipulative leaders, it's hard to believe there is righteous leadership in the church of God. Leadership that is self-less and receiving their direction from the throne room. After being under unrighteous leadership for so many years, I began to settle in my heart that this was the only type of leadership out there. I know it is crazy to think that God's true leaders would look like this, but when all that has been modeled in front of you is unrighteousness, you begin to settle for it. The church uses the excuse that no one is perfect. True, but that does not give an excuse for hellish behavior. I believe with all of my heart that righteous leadership is arising.

One of the greatest decisions my wife and I made was to connect and submit under the leadership of our parents in the faith and apostolic covering. They were just what we needed. My wife and I were in a place where we had totally given up on "coverings." Now being submitted under their leadership for the last few years, they are in no way shape or form like any other leader. Many leaders we had submitted to would show their colors and be more of a hindrance, but Apostle Steven & Dr. Melodye Hilton are the true examples of righteous leaders. Proverbs 29:2 says, "When the righteous are in authority the people rejoice, but when the wicked beareth rule the people mourn. In short, the best way to get the wicked from having any opportunity to lead is to stop following them and then model the righteous way.

There is a remnant of righteous leaders arising. Like me, they have seen the detriment of unrighteous leadership, because they have been victims of it. They have determined not to repeat what they have seen or experienced. One unfortunate thing I see often is the latter part of Proverbs 29:2, "The people mourn." The best way to dismantle this system or principality is not just to mourn, but to do something about it. My Apostle, Dr. Melodye, said it best, "Be angry, but do not sin." To be honest, I have a righteous anger within me that doesn't want injustice done to the people of God. The righteous leaders that are arising are driven and motivated by the love and justice of our God. We can no longer sit back and complain about Bishop so and so, and Apostle "Do-Wrong." While we are sitting back complaining, people are falling deeper into pits of darkness, and being chained down with unrighteousness and perversion. We must tell our story, and get in the posture of soldiers. Ready to contend for someone else's destiny. I fell into the web of unrighteous leadership, but I survived. There is an anointing and demand on my life to expose the deception and to lead others in freedom. I know I am not alone. If you are reading this, maybe you have a similar testimony or conviction to see the people of God in the fullness of safety. It is so disheartening to see the warfare that a believer deals with is due to unrighteousness from the hands of someone that calls their selves a leader.

The righteous that are arising will not compromise nor will they be lukewarm. We need people in the Kingdom of God that are not fearful but motivated to call a spade a spade, wrong, wrong, and right, right. We must regard honesty, truth, and justice as paramount virtues. "Isaiah 59:14-15 says, "And judgment standeth afar off: for truth is fallen in the street, and equity cannot enter. Yea, truth falleth; and he that departeth from evil maketh himself a prey and the Lord saw it, and it displeased him that there was no judgment. Western civilization culture has shifted into Pagan Mindsets. But the army of the righteous are purifying and restoring the image of Christianity in the land. Psalm 88:12 says, "Righteousness can no longer be done in the land of forgetfulness." I believe that as we restore the true motives of the church and put the attention back on Jesus, the righteous will be a force to be reckoned with. And the blueprint of the Kingdom will be our guide.

What does a righteous leader look like? When reading 9 Essential Qualities of a Godly leader by Brent Rinehart, a righteous leader carries themselves in the following ways:

- They seek God's direction
- They are modest, not arrogant
- They are a peacemaker
- They are fair and just
- They have honest, trustworthy counselors around them, and take heed to their words
- They are a good learner
- They are humble
- They are sensible and kind
- They are slow to anger

If you aren't following the above then you must question yourself are you a righteous leader, or better yet you must ask yourself if you leader is these attributes, the truth is if aren't then they are not righteous.

I talk about dancing with wolves throughout the book. It is so important that you keep your discernment on because as God is raising and releasing righteous leaders, the enemy is releasing false ones. We must turn on our discernment and recognize our leaders by their fruit in the pulpit and outside the pulpit. A major way that wolves manipulate the people of God is by playing off of their lack of knowledge of the word. The reality is a lot of people only open their word on Sunday or at church gatherings but never take the time to learn themselves. So whatever is coming out of the mouth of their leader they take it as the truth, this is dangerous. One can be easily manipulated if they don't know what the word says. So don't just study to show yourself approved, but study to keep yourself safe.

The enemy has perverted some of God's people to be wolves, but I believe in all of my heart that a new remnant of God-fearing righteous leaders is arising.

Prophetic Declaration: ***I decree and declare that there is a remnant of leaders that are arising. They shall carry themselves in the righteousness of God, and not be led by the perverted systems of old. They are releasing the very mind of Christ. New wine is being released through these vessels. This world will be turned upside down for the glory of God. These leaders will keep their face to the ground in reverence to God to seek direction from Him, their hearts and ears opened to hear the instructions of God. Their only mission is love, and from love, lives will be impacted, healed, transformed, and then released for Kingdom purpose.***

Chapter Eleven

The Greatest Gift

After years of abuse from spiritual leaders and rejection from love ones I truly felt like I deserved compensation for all that I had gone through. To be honest, some of the gifts I wanted to give them would probably not be Godly. I am reminded of one of my favorite scenes from the movie "The Help" where the maid Minny was tired of being misused by her boss Ms. Hilly, so she baked her famous pie. The pie was beautiful, and the boss was so happy with it. As the boss ate the pie and was enjoying the pie, the maid said, "Eat my sh*t." And as the lady continued to chew she realized that the pie she was enjoying was baked with the maid's feces in it. Now that's a gift you could provide the person that you worked so hard for, but they didn't appreciate you. Revenge is often what we think will make us feel better. Or is the immediate avenue for justice. The maid felt good as she ran out the door. That was her way of giving her resignation, but eventually that feeling of satisfaction because she got her back went away.

Let me tell you how I felt after going through all of the injustices that I went through. Remember the first injustice as a child that I perceived was rejection. I was my father's second child out of six. I always felt like he valued his two youngest children the most, so it made me angry. So I wanted to get back at my dad. So the best way I felt to get back at my dad was to speak evil of him. People would bring up my dad's name to me as I was growing up and I would literally curse his name. I would even say things like he is not my dad he is just a sperm donor. I would attempt to shut him out even when I would have to see him at family reunions. I would say to myself he hasn't been my dad all these years so why am I going to act like he is here. I would try to hurt his feelings so he would feel how I felt. I noticed as time progressed, it just made me feel worst.

How about my first male experience? I wanted this young man to feel how I felt. I blamed him even to his face that he was the reason I fell into homosexuality. As he progressed in ministry, I felt like it was my duty to bring harm to his reputation. People would ask me things about him, and I would tell them about his cheating ways, lying ways, and hypocritical ways. I didn't just stop there I even tried to bring my leader's reputation down along with his since they knew about what we were in but ignored it. I was angry. I felt like I was broken and it was everyone else's fault. But once again, I being spiteful was only destroying me. I remember sitting in my room and crying and crying saying how is everyone living their lives after they ruined mine. I got to the point where I once again attempted suicide. I felt I would never be happy so I might as well just die.

Time would progress, and I was so hurt that I even begin to curse the church that I came out of. That the church would be another Sodom and Gomorrah and everyone in there was going to die. I became a straight up witch with all of my spells and curses I was throwing at that church. Thinking in my mind karma is going to get these fools. I would even throw scriptures in there to justify how I felt, "they will reap what they sow.” I had to come to the realization that was not the heart or nature of God. As hard as it was, I had to realize that I had to change myself. I had to go through healing and from healing, find the greatest gift I could give which was forgiveness.

I could remember going to the grocery store or the mall and being afraid I would run into someone from my past. Sometimes, I thought about it so much that my thoughts became a reality, and I would run into the people that in my heart I truly hated. I would literally run to the next aisle or gave them my infamous stank face like don't even come over here. Anyone that knows me knows that my face tells it all. I am still working on that.

I even remember on a few instances years after the romantic relationship I had with the leader that we would cross each other's path in church services. I mean it was bound to happen; we both were still very active in ministry. I would see him, and he would get the microphone, and I would cringe. Even a friend told me that they noticed that while he was doing his "godly duties" in the pulpit that I was rolling my eyes. I will never forget when he came to me after a service to give me a hug, and I said, "Fool, don't you touch me." Why? I still hadn't forgiven.

Despite everything that I have gone through, I choose to give every rejecter, hater, abuser, and manipulator a gift of forgiveness. Forgiveness sure does not mean I have to sit with them at the kitchen table over a cup of tea and crumpets, but it does mean that I have to let what happened go. Free them and free myself. Even though we may not talk to or deal with our predator on a regular basis, I have found that at times they are very apologetic for what they have done, and may be so afraid of your reaction that they just don't verbally apologize or ask for forgiveness. Either way, forgive them, so you can live free and so they can as well. I am reminded of the story of Judas and Jesus. Judas was so distraught that he took his own life because he betrayed someone that he loved so much. Don't allow a person to kill themselves mentally, physically, or spiritually free them by forgiving them. Honestly, in my past, I wished those that hurt me would have killed themselves. But, I am reminded that God has given me so many chances and forgive me when I betrayed him by doing things my way rather than His. The greatest gift I received from Christ was forgiveness. And I understand that it is a blessing to give this to others. As you forgive, you must depend on the Holy Spirit. Within your own flesh, it is very difficult to forgive. Your flesh will bring into your remembrance everything that the person did to you. The Holy Spirit will cause you to pray for your enemies, and your cursing will shift into speaking blessings over the lives of those that have misused.

Luke 6:27-28Amplified Bible (AMP)

27 "But I say to you who hear [Me and pay attention to My words]: [a]Love [that is, unselfishly seek the best or higher good for] your enemies, [make it a practice to] do good to those who hate you, 28 bless *and* show kindness to those who curse you, pray for those who mistreat you.

To the wolves of my past, I could spend the rest of my life making a list of everything that you did to me, what you owe me, and how you made me feel, but that does no justice. So if you are one that has been in my past, and I am sure you know who you are. I can't give you a car as a gift, or money. I don't have a big gift with a big red shiny bow. I can tell you this gift is worth so much that the value cannot be determined. This gift is forgiveness from me to you. Also, use this gift to forgive yourself. If you haven't already, please get the deliverance you need, now that you know I have forgiven you wholeheartedly. Enjoy and live free.

Prophetic Declaration: ***I decree and declare that the people of God will release one of the greatest gifts that they can offer the gift of forgiveness. With this gift, we will see the dynamics of pain and shame shifted to people walking healed and even the accuser being made free. I declare that forgiveness is for both the forgiver and the forgiven. I declare and decree that when forgiveness is released the identity of a person changes. I decree and declare that people will not have a negative view of the church because of their past experiences by a church leader, but that as they release forgiveness in their hearts, the very essence of the church will be revealed to them. The church triumph is where we belong and who we are. Let forgiveness rain all across this world.***

Chapter Twelve

Deliverance Prayers

After reading this book, you may find yourself in a place where deliverance is needed, and you don't know how to go about it. I would recommend fasting and praying these prayer points to assist in bringing your breakthrough and freedom a reality.

Mark 9:29 KJV says, "He replied, This Kind can come forth by nothing, but prayer and fasting."

Use the below to break off all oppression of the enemy, so that you can see yourself free. I would also recommend doing praise and worship for about 10 minutes before starting your prayers to set an atmosphere for God's presence.

By the way, welcome to your day of Freedom!

Victim of Spiritual Abuse

Meditate: Psalm 119:134 "Redeem me from the oppression of man, that I may keep your precepts."

Prayer points:

- Father, I thank you that I am a survivor of every predator in my life
- I understand that my freedom is directly connected to my ability to wholeheartedly forgive my abuser
- I ask for forgiveness for any hatred towards my abuser (speak their name) that has manifested because of the hurt and pain I have endured
- I call on the fire of God to burn away any chord of unforgiveness, and bitterness in my life
- All residue be cleansed by the blood of Jesus
- I bind every word curse that has been spoken over my life by my abuser
- I loose angelic warriors to come to my aide to combat on my behalf
- Every demonic force assigned to my life God I declare that God has not given me a spirit of fear
- I rebuke you and declare that you are null and void in Jesus Name

- Any soul tie(s) that have been linked to me I call on the anointing of God to destroy every yoke
- Father, I bind any spirit that would cause me to repeat what has been done to me to someone else.
- I declare I am the righteousness of God

Spiritually Abuser

Meditate: Ezekiel 34: 2-3 "Son of Man, prophesy against the shepherds of Israel, prophesy, and say unto them, Thus saith the Lord God unto the shepherds; Woe be to the shepherds of Israel that do feed themselves! Should not the shepherds feed the flocks? Ye eat the fat, and ye clothe you with wool, ye kill them that are fed, but ye feed not the flock

Prayer points:

- Father, I honor you and identify my actions as an abuser and predator
- I confess my wrongdoings to those you have entrusted into my hands to serve and lead
- I will no longer use the excuse that it happened to me so that I can do it to others. Heal my soul Father!
- Father, forgive me for the abuse I inflicted upon your people and misuse of my authority

- I declare I will no longer lead by control and manipulation
- Spirit of perversion, you and all of your agents must leave now in the name of Jesus
- Lord, Your people, came to me for guidance and to be loved and I played on their vulnerability all for my own gain, make me new Lord and forgive me
- I command every spirit that dwells within me that causes me to exalt myself above God to be cast out in Jesus Name.
- I declare spiritual abuse in my bloodline stops here
- The fire of God, consume any generational patterns of spiritual abuse in my blood line and burn them away.
- Father, allow me to be transformed by the renewing of my mind.
- Anything that is trying to hide in me that could result in I turn on the light of the Spirit of God and expose you now. You are evicted out of my body, soul, and spirit.

Freedom from Religious spirit

Meditate: Ephesians 2:8-9 "For by grace are ye saved through faith; and that not of yourselves: it is the gift of God: Not of works, lest any man should boast."

Prayer points:

- Father, I identify and by your spirit confront the religious spirit that has been at work in my life and ministry
- Every connection and cord be severed now by the sword which is the word of the Lord
- I will no longer seek a platform
- I declare I'm no longer performance driven but purpose driven
- I recognize that for so long I have looked for the accolades and listened for the applause of man, but I now want nothing more than your spirit and for you to get the Glory
- Forgive me for seeking man and man-made opportunities, rather than you
- I bind the attention seeking, and I'm now available to create opportunities for man to see You
- Burn anything away from my life that does not look like or represent your Kingdom

- I understand your word in Proverbs 16:18 where it says, “Pride goes before destruction, a haughty spirit before a fall. Lord I humble myself and rid myself of all pride
- Every perverted agent at operation in my life I now expose you and declare you are not welcomed to house yourself in my soul
- I declare I am free from this bondage and have been made free by the redeeming blood of Jesus
- I will no longer mask my issues by playing church while my soul is in a condition for hell
- Make me more like you. In Jesus name, AMEN!

Spirit of Neediness

Meditate: Matthew 6:33 "But seek ye first the Kingdom of God, and his righteousness; all these things shall be added unto you

Prayer points:

- Father, there are voids in my life that I need to be filled
- I recognize that if I would take hold of you that I will be satisfied far beyond fleshly desires
- I declare that this hole inside of me will be filled

- You created me to be a vessel that needs pouring into. Send me your glory
- Send me the destiny links you have ordained for my life that will be effective to pour into me what is needed and call out what is not
- Lord, I am chasing after you wholeheartedly and your righteousness, fill me
- I come against the spirit that tells me that I will never experience fulfillment.
- I bind anything that is trying to take the place of you.
- I bind the need for money
- I bind the need for attention
- I bind the need for my flesh to be stroked by (anorexia, bulimia, bingeing, excessive fasting, self-mutilation, overeating, stealing, drug use, rage, criminal activity, nicotine abuse, alcohol, sexual sin, and perversion)
- I release a greater hunger and thirst after you
- I may have been rejected by a loved one that caused me to have a void, but I recognize you as the Father or Mother that I need
- I surrender to you, so fill me up and heal the wounds

- Occupy every part of me, In Jesus Name AMEN!

Slavery Mentality

Meditate: Galatians 5:1 "It was for freedom that Christ has set us free; therefore keep standing firm and do not be subject again to a yoke of slavery.

Prayer points:

- Father of Justice, let your Kingdom Come, and Your will be done
- I declare that I will no longer be in slavery to my leaders
- Give me a strong sense of discernment so that this will not continue as a cycle in my life
- I declare that my children and my children's children will not be bound by the wolves of religious organizations
- You have called your people to be free
- Restore my mind, as it has experienced turmoil and caused my decisions to be distorted
- I recognize that you called me to submit to my senior leaders but not be manipulated to be their personal property or their slave
- Restore my identity in You

- I declare and decree that you are healing the spiritual wounds that I obtained from my spiritual slave owner
- There are no more chains holding me
- Father restore my perception of your people
- Forgive me for releasing hate in my heart for all leaders because of the behavior of one leader (If you are a leader that needs deliverance from being a slave master continue and pray the below)
- I also recognize that not only am I not a slave, but my identity does not call me to be a slave master
- This spirit stops with me
- I will not lead by intimidation
- I will not use religion and distort the word of God to control those that I lead
- Father this spirit is exposed and no longer at work in me or around me in Jesus Name
- Thank you for freedom today and forevermore, AMEN!

Taking Off the Victim Mentality

Meditate: Philippians 4:8 "Finally, brethren, whatsoever things are true, whatsoever things [are] honest, whatsoever things [are] just, whatsoever things [are] pure, whatsoever things [are] lovely, whatsoever things [are] good report; if [there be] any virtue, and if [there be] any praise, think on these things."

Prayer points:

- Lord, I thank you that I am not conformed to what I have experienced but transformed to what you have ordained
- Victim mentality I declare that you will no longer inflict physical or emotional pain on me
- I will no longer accept what I went through to make excuses for having a victim mentality
- I have been made in your image, and I recognize that your promises are still yea and amen
- Even with this victim mentality I recognize that the jealousy spirit has also shown up in my heart
- I will no longer be jealous because I will have what you have said
- I bind the self- pity spirit

- Father, I choose to forgive those who have used me, hurt me and abused me
- I tear up the note that I have pinned from the emotions of heart filled with hate
- I repent for not acknowledging the areas that I was weak that lead me into a vulnerable place to be a victim
- I repent on behalf of myself and my ancestors for accepting abusive treatment as if it was normal and it was just the way things had to be
- I even come against the result of my abuse causing my motives of telling my story to get attention
- Today is my day of freedom, and I am no longer a victim, by the power of the Holy Spirit, AMEN!

Conclusion

My prayer is that those that are dancing with wolves will eventually come to the place of awakening, like the young man we met at the beginning of the book. Unfortunately, this was not a fiction book but called out real accounts and facts to bring true awareness to what may be happening behind the doors of some of our favorite churches. Some people's story did not end like mine where they had an opportunity to stop the dancing and confront the spirit. Some have died physically, or are still alive but are dealing with the mental effects of being abused by their beloved leader.

There is still hope for the church today. The late Bishop G.E. Patterson of the Church of God in Christ would always declare, be delivered, be healed, and be set free. At the end of the day, this applies to the wolves and to those that have been afflicted. I believe in my heart of hearts that God is freeing both the captor and the captive.

As for the young man that you met at the beginning of the book, I am better than I have ever been. I am experiencing the grace of God and walking out my freedom each and every day. I often think of where I would be today if I had never stopped dancing with wolves. Even if I was still alive what would I be like, where would I be, and what would be going on? Well, I am thankful that I am delivered, healed, and free. I have a beautiful anointed wife, 3 called out children, a thriving ministry, and even making an impact in the marketplace.

Oh and in case you wanted to know, I am still dancing, and I welcome you to dance along with me. It is a freedom dance that comes from the Holy Spirit. Join with me as we connect across the world and demolish the spirit of abuse.

Made in the USA
Middletown, DE
15 May 2017